Homo Sapiens

A Captivating Guide to the History of Humans and Human Evolution

Free Bonus from Captivating History (Available for a Limited time)

Hi History Lovers!

Now you have a chance to join our exclusive history list so you can get your first history ebook for free as well as discounts and a potential to get more history books for free! Simply visit the link below to join.

Captivatinghistory.com/ebook

Also, make sure to follow us on Facebook, Twitter and Youtube by searching for Captivating History.

Table of Contents

Introduction – The Story of Our Species

There is a species on Earth unlike any other: *Homo sapiens*. It is not the strongest nor the most numerous in numbers, but it shows a remarkable ability for survival. The story of our species started about 200,000 years ago in Africa. *Homo sapiens* have since spread around the world, developed new technologies, and not only survived but also thrived.

Modern scientific studies have revealed a lot about the origins of our species and how it developed. Today, we know that *Homo sapiens* first evolved in Africa and then spread around the world over thousands of years. Early humans faced towering glaciers and treacherous landscapes, but their unwavering spirit pushed them forward. In the ancient caves of Europe, we can find troves of artwork left behind by our ancestors. These stunning depictions created tens of thousands of years ago reveal a deeply ingrained urge to communicate and express oneself through art.

We also know about numerous older species of early humans that existed even before *Homo sapiens* emerged. While *Homo sapiens* is the only human species existing today, it was not always like this. In the distant past, *Homo sapiens* shared the world with several other human species. They sometimes even interbred, which reflects in our genes today. We will uncover the fascinating stories locked within their DNA, revealing interbreeding events and shared ancestry that intertwine us with these ancient cousins.

Compared to many other animals, *Homo sapiens* is not a strong species. We cannot see in the dark, and we lack the strength and speed of efficient predators. However, *Homo sapiens* possesses numerous traits that helped it to survive and become extremely successful as a species. It is all thanks to the cognitive capabilities that we developed during the course of evolution. Furthermore, our social abilities and communication skills have allowed us to build communities for strength and protection. From the discovery of fire to the mastery of metalworking, our ancestors were relentless inventors. They harnessed the power of the elements, shaping tools and weapons that allowed them to tame the wild and conquer new frontiers.

This book traces the evolution of *Homo sapiens*, first through earlier forms of proto-humans and early humans that predate our species. After this, we will trace the emergence of our species, *Homo sapiens*. Discover a time known as the Agricultural Revolution, and witness a profound shift in the way *Homo sapiens* lived. Our ancestors were no longer reliant solely on hunting and gathering; instead, they began to cultivate the land, domesticate animals, and establish settled communities. We will witness the invention of agriculture and talk about all of the different biological and cultural factors that made *Homo sapiens* so resistant as a species.

Book Organization

In Chapter 1, we will talk about early evolution leading to the emergence of *Homo sapiens*. Did you know that not all proto-humans were our direct ancestors? We will talk about what happened to the other ones and the evolutionary line that led to the emergence of *Homo sapiens*. The chapter will also cover the importance of walking on two feet and how it originally contributed more to the evolution than the size of the brain.

Chapter 2 focuses on the emergence of *Homo sapiens*. You will see that there were different species that fall into this category. We will talk about their development and how our own species, *Homo sapiens sapiens*, finally emerged in Africa. There is an important difference between the archaic *Homo sapiens* and anatomically modern humans, which we will cover. For simplicity's sake, the book will continue to refer to our species as "*Homo sapiens*" for the rest of the text.

In Chapter 3, we will talk more about the relationship between our species and other human species before they died out. Did modern humans and Neanderthals interbreed? Who were the Denisovans? Is it true that our species is responsible for the disappearance of the Neanderthals?

Chapter 4 talks about the large migrations of *Homo sapiens*. Unlike previous species, who only moved to Eurasia, *Homo sapiens* crossed further distances. We will learn how our species reached the Americas, thanks to the Bering land bridge during the Ice Age, and how it populated the far corners of Australia and Oceania.

In Chapter 5, we describe different tools that prehistoric humans used for survival. Tool use is one of the defining characteristics of being human, and we will explore the stone technologies that early humans used for hunting, building shelters, and defending themselves. Did you know that different human species can sometimes be recognized by their different technologies? We will also talk about the role of fire and cooking food for prehistoric humans.

Chapter 6 focuses on the development of thought and language. How did *Homo sapiens* learn to communicate in such an effective way, and how does language help in survival? What are some specific aspects of thought and cognition that helped the evolution of early humans?

In Chapter 7, we will talk about the importance of culture. You will learn that it wouldn't be possible for our species to survive without specific learned strategies of survival and socialization.

Chapter 8 focuses on the invention of agriculture and animal domestication. We will talk about the importance of these inventions for *Homo sapiens*. How did human lives change with agriculture? Was there a Neolithic Revolution, or is that a myth?

In Chapter 9, we will talk about the first human cities and the rise of the first states. What is the importance of complex societies, and how did they contribute to increasing inequalities among different groups? How was writing invented, and how did it change the world? We will also cover the importance of warfare, religion, and science for early human states.

Chapter 10 focuses on biological and cultural diversity today. What are the key similarities and differences between different *Homo sapiens* groups? What is cultural diversity, and how does one species have so many cultural differences? We will also talk about the biological unity of humankind and the various adaptations that our species have developed.

To start, let us go back seven million years ago. We are in Africa witnessing something remarkable: a group of primates starting to walk upright. This is how the story of our species begins.

Chapter 1 – Early Evolution

Homo sapiens is the only surviving human species on our planet today. However, we should look into the past to meet the others that are now extinct. We need to understand the millions of years of human evolution. This is where our story starts, with the first divergence from the common ancestor that we share with chimpanzees. Many of these early proto-humans were not our direct ancestors, but they are important to understand human evolution.

What does *Homo sapiens* mean? The word *Homo* means "human" or "man" in Latin, while *sapiens* means "wise." Humans have their place alongside other animals and living beings. This biological classification for organizing the living world dates back to the 18th century. Swedish botanist and zoologist Carl Linnaeus is responsible for developing an effective system to classify all living things. He was also the one who developed the binominal nomenclature, a system for scientifically naming species that is still used today. In this system, a scientific name consists of the name of the species and genus (a taxonomic rank above the species).

Fun fact: Linnaeus is the one who first classified our species as *Homo sapiens*. It is easy to understand why. *Homo* is the name of the genus, and *sapiens* is the name of the species.

We can understand the process of human evolution if we start with the place of *Homo sapiens* among other animals. We know that humans belong to the order of primates, along with other apes and monkeys. The first proto-primates date back to about seventy million years in the past, before the extinction of dinosaurs. Modern primates first appeared around fifty-five million years ago. Not all primates are similar to us. Primates closest to humans include great apes, and they appeared more recently. The great apes are orangutans, gorillas, and chimpanzees, our closest animal relatives. Scientists estimate that a shared ancestor of humans and chimpanzees lived around six to seven million years ago.

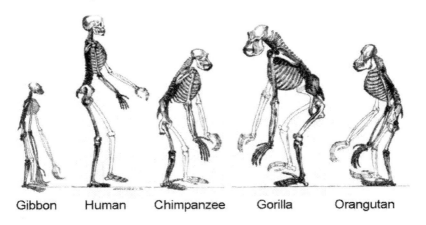

Gibbon   Human   Chimpanzee   Gorilla   Orangutan

A look at the skeletons of humans and primates.
https://commons.wikimedia.org/wiki/File:Ape_skeletons.png

Within the primate family, two significant groups are worth mentioning. The first is the genus *Pan*, encompassing the two living species of chimpanzees: common chimpanzees and bonobos. The other one is the branch of the hominins, which includes proto-humans, early humans, and our own species, *Homo sapiens*.

Hominins are a specific group of primates that first emerged around six to seven million years ago. Evolutionarily, they encompass all species closer to humans than to chimpanzees. Modern scientific studies indicate that hominins were a remarkably diverse group, with different species coexisting or even interbreeding at certain points. Amidst this diversity, only one species survives today: *Homo sapiens*.

There are many traces of early humans. Archaeologists have found their tools and fossils. Fossils are remains of living organisms found in nature. Fossils can provide crucial information about plants and animals from the past, including early humans. They can be used to prove the presence of proto-humans and early humans in a place. The problem? Fossils are fragile, so not all of them are preserved. Additionally, there are many fossils out there still waiting to be discovered.

Charles Darwin first suggested the African origin of modern humans. He observed that *Homo sapiens* had more physical similarities to African apes than to primates from other parts of the world. Modern science proved this theory through genetic research. Early evolutionists of the late 19th and early 20th centuries believed that the distinctive characteristic that set us apart from other apes was the brain. They proposed that human evolution began with a rapid increase in brain size, leading to improved intelligence in our ancestors. Improved intelligence allowed early humans to develop the use of tools, speeding up the process of evolution. According to these beliefs, it was the brain that developed first, with the rest of the body following. Scientists working with these theories assumed that early humans would have ape-like bodies but much larger brains.

Today, we know that the opposite happened. What marked the beginning of hominin evolution was not so much the increase in brain size but changes in movement, namely starting to walk upright. While brain size remained modest and increased slowly, walking upright is what set hominins apart from their primate relatives.

Bipedalism (walking upright) played an important role in the evolution of hominins. It has been theorized that walking on two legs helped human ancestors in numerous ways. First, it was an efficient way of moving because it saved energy compared to primates who walk on four legs. Also, bipedalism is helpful for noticing potential dangers and food. And it left hands free to do other tasks, such as using tools.

Let us begin with the earliest hominins, the species that started the development of bipedalism around six to seven million years ago in Africa.

Early Hominins

Who were the earliest hominins? Scientists label primate fossils as hominins if there are signs of developing bipedalism. Among the earliest hominins, scientists recognize several species today:

- *Sahelanthropus tchadensis* (7 million years ago), found in Chad;

- *Orrorin tugenensis* (6-5.7 million years ago), found in Kenya;

- *Ardipithecus kadabba* (5.8-5.2 million years ago), found in Ethiopia;

- *Ardipithecus ramidus* (4.5-4 million years ago), found in Ethiopia.

This wide territory across Africa indicates that the earliest hominins occupied a larger territory than it was originally thought. Most of the earliest fossils are highly fragmented, so it is not easy to reconstruct the physical appearance of the species or their abilities. These first hominins were not humans, but they display traces of a crucial characteristic for all proto-humans: bipedalism.

The first human ancestors were arboreal (tree dwellers), just like the majority of primates. The main difference is that hominins could walk upright for longer periods of time. We are not sure why early hominins developed bipedalism. Some scientists suggest that this occurred because of changes in climate, which triggered the disappearance of large forests in East Africa. Unsurprisingly, this had a dramatic effect. Large forests were replaced by savannahs and woodlands, which are very different types of environments. The problem with this theory? The fossil records indicate that many of the early hominins actually lived in areas full of trees, which means that theory doesn't explain the emergence of bipedalism.

How do we know that hominins walked upright if we do not have their complete skeletons? Yes, skeleton fragmentation is a big problem. Luckily, there are certain characteristics that can point to bipedalism. These features offer valuable clues about the movement and posture of our early human ancestors. The most important characteristics are the shape and angle of the pelvis and the position of the big toe. The angle at which the femur (thigh bone) connects to the hip joint can reveal whether an organism walked on two legs. In bipeds, the femur angles inward toward the knee, facilitating a more efficient stride and weight distribution. Fossils displaying these distinctive femur angles suggest adaptations for bipedal locomotion. The structure of foot bones is another crucial characteristic in identifying bipedalism. The feet exhibit specific features, such as an arched foot, a robust heel bone (calcaneus), and a non-opposable big toe aligned with the other toes. These adaptations enhance balance, shock absorption, and efficient forward momentum. Fossil footprints can also provide valuable evidence of early hominin bipedalism.

Another important indicator for walking upright is the position of the opening on the base of the skull (foramen magnum). This opening is located closer to the middle in bipedal species instead of the back, as can be found in non-bipedal species. Bipedalism requires adjustments in the spinal column to maintain an upright posture. In humans, the lumbar region of the spine exhibits inward curvature (lordosis) to support the weight of the upper body. Fossil vertebral remains that display similar spinal curvatures suggest adaptations for bipedal walking. Keep in mind that early hominins did not fully exhibit all of these traits the way later ones did, but fossil records indicate changes took place, which signals the beginnings of bipedalism among early hominins.

The early hominins' transition to bipedalism, cognitive advancements, tool use, dietary adaptations, environmental flexibility, and social behaviors set the stage for our species' subsequent evolution and success. Understanding the characteristics and ecological context of these early hominins is crucial for unraveling the intricate tapestry of our human ancestry.

We can't call all of these species human ancestors because *Homo sapiens* did not directly evolve from all of them. Some of the early hominin species died out without leaving traces of further evolution into new species. However, some evolved into distinctive forms of other hominins. Scientists believe that a specific species called *Ardipithecus* evolved around 4.5 million years ago into a distinctive group of hominins: *Australopithecus*.

Australopithecus

Australopithecus includes numerous species that are important for understanding human evolution. While these are still not members of our own genus, *Homo* (humans), some of them did evolve into the earliest members of the genus *Homo*. *Australopithecus* is a genus involving several species of fully bipedal hominins. Their presence was found in East and South Africa. *Australopithecus* provides fascinating proof of early bipedalism through a remarkable find of 3.7- to 3.6-million-year-old footprints preserved in volcanic ash at the Laetoli site (Tanzania). The footprints of three individuals clearly show the shape of the feet, which indicates bipedalism.

The most famous *Australopithecus* species is *Australopithecus afarensis*, which lived about four to three million years ago. This hominin includes probably the best-known human fossil: Lucy. Lucy (or Dinkinesh, her name in Amharic) was a young female individual discovered in the 1970s in Ethiopia. She lived about 3.2 million years ago. Lucy was fully bipedal, although her curved fingers and toes are evidence of tree climbing.

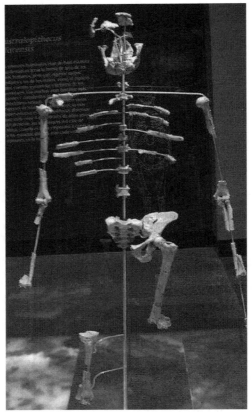

A cast of Lucy's skeleton.
https://commons.wikimedia.org/wiki/File:Lucy_Mexico.jpg

Australopithecus afarensis is important because it is the best candidate for a human ancestor, at least according to present knowledge. Scientists suggest that some of the *Australopithecus* moved toward becoming exclusively bipedal, which triggered the development of more effective forms of walking upright.

The First Humans

This is how, around 2.8 to 2.5 million years ago, the first members of the genus *Homo* first appeared. These are still not our species, *Homo sapiens*, but they are hominins belonging to our genus. The genus is a biological rank (category) consisting of different yet closely related species. All of the early members of the genus *Homo* can be classified as humans.

But how is this determined? What are specific human characteristics that would make a hominin fall into this category? In general, the defining characteristics of the genus *Homo* include larger brains, smaller teeth, and more extensive use of tools.

For the longest time, scientists believed that only humans (genus *Homo*) were able to make and use tools. This idea has been abandoned. We know of toolmakers who were not likely to belong to the genus *Homo*. The oldest stone tools that we know about are estimated to be 3.3 to 3.5 million years old. They were found in Kenya. Of course, the oldest tools so far recovered do not necessarily mean the oldest ever; it is possible that, in the future, even older ones will be discovered. However, the presence of these handmade tools tells us about the existence of toolmakers. They were probably *Australopithecus*.

However, it is notable that the members of the genus *Homo* were the ones who developed more tools. It is possible to conclude that they used tools regularly in everyday life and that toolmaking was an important aspect of these species' abilities. Some of the earliest stone tools made by early humans were found in Olduvai Gorge in Tanzania, and they are about 2.5 million years old. These stone tools are known as the Oldowan tradition of stone tools.

Another important feature of all human species is complete bipedalism. While the *Australopithecus* species were bipedal, the mechanics of their walk was still imperfect compared to later species, particularly those in the genus *Homo*.

What was the first human species? The earliest member of the genus *Homo* is *Homo habilis*, who lived about 2.8 to 1.5 million years ago, mostly in southeastern Africa. The species name means "handy man" and refers to the use of tools. These early humans had a relatively small brain capacity compared to our species, but it was larger than that of the *Australopithecus*.

Homo habilis fossils were found in Koobi Fora in Kenya. These remains show interesting features. For instance, we learn that these hominins had similar body proportions to *Australopithecus afarensis*, with the main difference being the increased brain size. It also showed signs of more complete bipedalism. Another early human, *Homo rudolfensis*, lived in East Africa around 2.5 to 1.5 million years ago, and it was much more robust than *Homo habilis* and had a slightly larger brain capacity.

Homo ergaster and *Homo erectus*

Homo erectus is among the best-known species of early humans, along with the Neanderthals (more about them in Chapters 2 and 3). There is a simple yet important reason for the popularity of *Homo erectus*: many fossils. Unlike earlier species, *Homo erectus* remains were found throughout Africa and even in China and Indonesia. There is plenty of evidence demonstrating that *Homo erectus* was a long-living species (in fact, one of the longest-living of them all). They appeared around 1.9 million years ago and disappeared around 100,000 years ago, at a time when *Homo sapiens* already existed! This hominin displays more human-like traits in body proportions and skull appearance. Also, its brain size was larger than earlier species.

The Turkana Boy, an example of a Homo erectus.

Before the emergence of *Homo erectus*, there was an earlier form, *Homo ergaster*. It is sometimes known as "early African *Homo erectus*" since its later forms are known as *Homo erectus*, especially when talking about fossils from Eurasia. Fossil remains of *Homo ergaster* have been discovered at several sites, including Koobi Fora and Lake Turkana in Kenya, as well as Olduvai Gorge in Tanzania.

Scientists are still unsure whether *Homo ergaster* and *Homo erectus* are the same species or are simply closely related. We know that *Homo ergaster* is older, and many scientists assume that this species gradually evolved into *Homo erectus* around two million years ago. However, there is no consensus about these claims. It is today accepted that modern humans evolved directly from African forms of *Homo erectus* (*Homo ergaster*). What is important to know about *Homo ergaster*? This early human had smaller teeth than previous hominins, as well as a slightly increased brain size. However, the brain size increase was not particularly significant. Today, we know that a larger brain size was not the main sign of human evolution.

Homo ergaster and *Homo erectus* seem to be the oldest hominins who used fire. The evidence for this comes from numerous burned areas associated with this hominin, some of them older than one million years. Unfortunately, it is not possible to tell whether this was a natural fire or a human-made one. *Homo erectus* used fire to cook food, which might have impacted human evolution. There is a possibility that *Homo erectus* was a hunter. It is also possible that these early humans were scavengers, taking leftover meat from animals previously killed by other predators.

Remember the Laetoli footprints? They are not the only hominin footprints that we know of. A more recent set of footprints found in Ileret (Kenya), dating to about 1.5 million years ago, provide proof of a species completely adapted to walking and running on two legs. These footprints are likely to belong to a human species known as *Homo ergaster*. This species provides evidence of hunting and toolmaking.

Homo ergaster is associated with the Acheulean stone tool industry, which represents a significant technological advancement compared to the earlier Oldowan tools. Acheulean tools were more refined and standardized, often characterized by bifacial (flaked on both sides) hand axes and cleavers. This suggests an increased sophistication in toolmaking abilities and potentially more complex cultural and behavioral patterns. *Homo erectus* is also known for these Acheulian stone tools. These tools gradually replaced the earlier Oldowan tools in the archaeological record.

Acheulean tools are very distinctive. The most common form was a multifunctional hand ax. These tools have a specific shape, and they are found throughout all the territories occupied by *Homo erectus*. *Homo erectus* likely used these tools for various activities, such as butchering meat, woodworking, and processing plant materials. The sophistication of their tool technology indicates an enhanced ability to exploit their environment and suggests more complex cognitive and behavioral abilities.

Homo ergaster and *Homo erectus* likely lived in social groups and engaged in complex social behaviors. The presence of Acheulean tools suggests a shared culture and the transmission of knowledge and skills within their communities. The ability to control fire provided *Homo erectus* with numerous advantages, such as protection from predators, warmth, and the ability to cook food. Cooking would have had profound effects on their diet and overall energy availability. Cooking increases the ease of digestion, unlocking more nutrients and reducing the time and effort required for chewing.

Around this time, early humans explored new territories, first in Africa and then outside of it. Contemporary scientists believe that the earliest migrations out of Africa happened 2 to 1.5 million years ago. We know of these migrations because of the presence of human fossils and tools in Eurasia. For example, some of the oldest human tools found outside of Africa are located in China and date back to about two million years ago.

But what about the oldest fossils outside of Africa? The oldest fossils that we know of are a bit younger, about 1.8 million years old, and are found in Dmanisi (Georgia). Stone tools found at Dmanisi resemble stone tools found in Africa. It is assumed that they were made by the same or very similar species. These human remains resemble African *Homo ergaster* but are also different in some crucial elements. Scientists are not completely sure whether these humans belonged to *Homo habilis* or to a local form of *Homo erectus*.

What we do know is that traces of *Homo erectus* were found around Eurasia. In Indonesia and Java, the evidence is about 1.6 million years old, while the oldest in Europe is about 1.5 million years old. Fossils are typically a bit younger. The reason? Stone tools are stronger and can be preserved in the environment more easily than human remains. The earliest European fossils date to about 1.4 million years ago, first in southern Europe (Spain and Italy) and to around 800 000 years ago farther north in the European continent.

Homo erectus holds immense significance in the narrative of human evolution. Furthermore, the cultural advancements demonstrated by *Homo erectus*, such as tool use, fire control, and potentially cooking, were critical in shaping the trajectory of human evolution. *Homo erectus* spread out of Africa, and it endured numerous challenges over its 1.5 million years of existence. In fact, *Homo erectus* is, by far, the longest-living of all human relatives; still, they eventually died out around 100,000 to 70,000 years ago. They were replaced by a new group of humans: *Homo sapiens.*

Chapter 2 – Homo Sapiens Emerges

Around 700,000 to 600,000 years ago, the uniform *Homo erectus* fossil record disappeared. While *Homo erectus* still existed as a species, it was not alone, as new humans started to appear in Africa. The gradual appearance of more varied human fossils, first in Africa and then in Asia and Europe, has been noted. These fossils are known under the collective name "archaic *Homo sapiens*," typically labeled by one distinctive species: *Homo heidelbergensis*. This is an important species for understanding human evolution, as scientists believe that *Homo heidelbergensis* is a shared ancestor of Neanderthals and our own species.

A quick digression. The full scientific name of our species is not simply *Homo sapiens* but *Homo sapiens sapiens* (*sapiens* appears twice in the name). It is the only surviving member of the *Homo sapiens* group. Before the emergence of our species, the archaic forms of *Homo sapiens* roamed the Earth, first in Africa and then in Eurasia. To understand the story of our species, we need to know how it relates to the earlier forms of *Homo sapiens*.

Archaic *Homo sapiens*

Who was the archaic *Homo sapiens*? In general, this is an umbrella term for different species of early *Homo sapiens*. Modern research in genetics, biological anthropology, and archaeology reveals the full origins of our species. Today, we know that modern humans first evolved in Africa and that they evolved from the earlier human species present on the continent. While East Africa has been traditionally regarded as the primary point of origin, recent studies suggest a gradual evolution throughout the entire continent. Remarkably, the earliest known fossil evidence of *Homo sapiens* originates from multiple African sites.

Archaic *Homo sapiens* encompass various regional populations, each displaying unique characteristics and adaptations. In Africa, *Homo heidelbergensis* is a prominent example of an archaic human species. Fossils from sites such as Bodo and Kabwe provide valuable insights into their morphology and behavior. *Homo heidelbergensis* had a robust build and large braincases and showed advancements in tool manufacturing and cognitive abilities.

Scientists today believe that *Homo sapiens* evolved from *Homo heidelbergensis*, which itself evolved from *Homo ergaster* or *Homo erectus*. There is a gap in the fossil record from 500,000 to about 250,000 years ago, which makes it difficult to fully reconstruct the evolution of modern humans. *Homo heidelbergensis*, the probable direct predecessor to our species, remains largely unfamiliar to the general population.

Homo heidelbergensis displayed a number of distinct anatomical features. They had a larger brain capacity than their predecessors, with an average cranial capacity falling between that of *Homo erectus* and modern humans. Their skull morphology featured a prominent brow ridge but a flatter face than those of earlier human species. *Homo heidelbergensis* had a more modern body structure compared to earlier hominins. They possessed a larger and more robust skeleton, indicating greater strength and endurance. The limb proportions were similar to modern humans, with long legs and shorter arms, suggesting a more efficient bipedal gait.

A model of the head of Homo heidelbergensis.

These ancient humans were skilled toolmakers, producing a wide range of tools using techniques such as bifacial flaking. Their tools show advancements in technology and adaptability to various environments. This ability to create and use tools likely contributed to their success in hunting, scavenging, and gathering resources. *Homo heidelbergensis* also exhibited evidence of controlled use of fire. This ability to harness fire provided them with warmth, protection, and the ability to cook food, which offered nutritional and social advantages.

Archaic *Homo sapiens* contributed to the cultural and technological advancements of our lineage. They developed more sophisticated tool industries, improved hunting strategies, and exhibited social and cooperative behaviors. The presence of symbolic artifacts and evidence of ritualistic practices suggests the beginnings of complex cognitive abilities and symbolic expression.

Homo heidelbergensis evolved in Africa, probably from *Homo ergaster*. Like *Homo erectus, Homo heidelbergensis* migrated to Eurasia. They expanded their range across different environments, adapting to diverse climates and resource availability. The successful migration and colonization of regions outside of Africa laid the groundwork for the subsequent evolution of distinct regional populations.

Fun fact: *Homo heidelbergensis* interbred with earlier species of humans who were already living in these territories. Later, *Homo heidelbergensis* evolved into a distinctive species, the Neanderthals.

In Asia, archaic *Homo sapiens* include groups such as the Denisovans, known from fragmentary fossils found in Siberia's Denisova Cave. This is a newly discovered (2010) species, and you can read more about them in Chapter 3. The discovery of their DNA in modern humans highlights interbreeding events between archaic and modern *Homo sapiens* populations. Interbreeding between close species of early humans was not a rare thing and was practiced by many groups, including our own species once it developed and moved out of Africa.

The Neanderthals

Homo neanderthalensis, better known as the Neanderthals, is a distinctive species of early humans. They are the first discovered humans other than our own species and were found in the early to mid-19th century. The first findings were not recognized as early humans, but a discovery from 1859 in Feldhofer Cave of the Neander Valley (Germany) was. Originally, Neanderthals were considered to be inferior beings who were barely bipedal. Today, we know that the Neanderthals had numerous similarities with our own species.

The Neanderthals lived primarily in Europe and western and central Asia (such as Syria and Iraq). The earliest fossils date to about 400,000 to 300,000 years ago. Neanderthals are recognizable in the fossil record due to their pronounced brow ridge, sturdy bodies, and brain size that is actually larger than that of modern humans.

A reconstruction of a Neanderthal man.

Neanderthals had a robust skeletal structure, with thick bones and muscular bodies that helped them endure the physical demands of their environment. They had a barrel-shaped chest, which likely aided in their respiratory capacity and provided additional support for their upper body strength.

Neanderthals also exhibited adaptations to cold weather. They had a stocky build, shorter limbs, and a broader pelvis compared to modern humans. These features helped them conserve body heat in colder climates, as well as enhance their strength for activities like hunting and gathering.

Relying on the available evidence of stone tools and bones, which constitute the majority of our knowledge about this distant era, we can make reasonable assumptions about Neanderthal social life. They exhibited increasing sophistication, which enabled them to form stronger bonds and larger social units, ultimately enhancing their chances of survival.

According to the social brain hypothesis, the increasing complexity of social skills necessary to navigate human groups likely drove the evolutionary expansion of brain size observed from the earliest *Homo* species. It created a positive feedback loop where larger social groups demanded more cognitive processing power for individuals to thrive, leading to even greater complexity. This challenge of managing complex social relations applied to both the Neanderthals and *Homo sapiens*, the two primary descendants of *Homo heidelbergensis*. This may explain why both populations continued to evolve larger brains and, consequently, larger group sizes in tandem with each other.

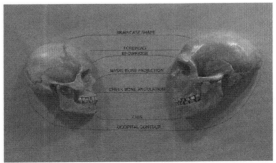

Comparison between Homo sapiens (left) and Neanderthals (right).
hairymuseummatt (original photo), KaterBegemot (derivative work), CC BY-SA 2.0

Neanderthals probably had slightly smaller social networks than early *Homo sapiens sapiens* groups (around 100 to 150 individuals). These networks were likely structured similarly to modern hunter-gatherer groups.

The life of the Neanderthals is inseparable from the ice ages (yes, there were several!). The interplay of the ice age cycles and their impact on solar radiation and climate change shaped the environment in which the Neanderthals thrived and eventually declined.

The Neanderthals were intelligent and compassionate beings. They demonstrated burial practices, which, according to current knowledge, make them the earliest known humans to engage in such rituals. This provides evidence of Neanderthal behavior and thoughts, as well as the existence of altruism. Their burial practices provide insights into their complex cognitive abilities and social behaviors, highlighting their remarkable similarities to modern humans.

Research has provided valuable insights into Neanderthals' cognitive capacities and sheds light on their mental capabilities. Neanderthals demonstrated several advanced mental abilities. They possessed a relatively large brain size comparable to modern humans, suggesting the potential for sophisticated cognitive processing. Brain size alone does not reveal much information. However, there is evidence of large-scale cooperative hunting and the development of more sophisticated stone tools. These advancements indicate a significant shift in the behavior of early Neanderthals. The revolutionary nature of these developments, which distinguished the Neanderthals from their *Homo heidelbergensis* ancestors and set them apart from other human species, is often overlooked. One notable area that provided an advantage to Neanderthals was their social relations, enabling them to increase group size and expand their range. Larger brains could also have contributed to improved food procurement through more efficient hunting.

Collectively, evidence, such as brain size, bone morphology, group hunting, and stone tool technology, allows us to identify 250,000 years ago as a significant moment marking the full emergence of the Neanderthals.

Originally, scientists believed that the Neanderthals were the direct ancestors of modern humans. According to that theory, *Homo sapiens* evolved from the Neanderthals sometime in the last 100,000 years. However, later research proved that *Homo sapiens* is not a direct descendant of the Neanderthals and that these two species coexisted. There are varying perspectives among scientists.

The leading ideas:

1. *Homo neanderthalensis.* This theory postulates that the Neanderthals and *Homo sapiens sapiens* are different but closely related species of humans.

2. *Homo sapiens neanderthalensis.* This theory claims that the Neanderthals and modern humans are two different varieties of the same *Homo sapiens* species, *Homo sapiens neanderthalensis* and *Homo sapiens sapiens*, respectively.

There is still no answer as to which of these two theories is correct. What we do know is that our species are very closely related and interbred with each other. We will examine the relationship between the two species in the next chapter.

Homo Sapiens Sapiens

Finally, we get to our own species, scientifically called *Homo sapiens sapiens*. In the rest of this book, we will refer to our species simply as *Homo sapiens*, but we need to understand its difference from earlier human forms.

The cranium (skull) of early modern humans exhibits several distinguishing features. Compared to earlier hominin species, their skulls are characterized by a high rounded braincase with a prominent forehead. This development signifies an expansion in brain size, although our skulls are smaller than those of Neanderthals. Additionally, the face of early modern humans is relatively flat, with reduced brow ridges compared to earlier hominins.

Another distinctive skeletal trait found in early modern humans is a reduced brow ridge or brow ridge projection. Compared to earlier human species, early modern humans exhibit a less pronounced and more slender brow ridge. This reduction in brow ridge prominence contributes to the verticality of the forehead and creates a more delicate facial appearance.

Early modern humans also possessed a more slender and retracted face compared to previous human species. Their faces are characterized by a smaller and more tucked-in mid-face region, including the nasal area. This retraction of the face created a flatter facial profile compared to the more protruding faces observed in archaic humans like

Neanderthals.

The teeth of early modern humans reveal important adaptations. Compared to their ancestors, they possess smaller and weaker teeth. The reduction in tooth size, especially in the canines and molars, indicates changes in dietary habits, possibly due to the introduction of food processing techniques and advancements in tool use.

The skeletons of early modern humans also exhibit distinct features. They generally have a more slender skeletal structure compared to their predecessors, like Neanderthals. The pelvis of anatomically modern humans is broad and bowl-shaped, which aids in the birth of large-brained infants.

Overall, the skeletal features of early *Homo sapiens sapiens* reflect anatomical adaptations that contributed to their success as a species. These traits, including the high forehead, reduced brow ridge, retracted face, dental changes, prominent chin, and gracile postcranial skeleton, provide insights into the evolutionary trajectory of our species and the unique characteristics that define us as anatomically modern humans.

The earliest *Homo sapiens sapiens* fossils come from Morocco (Jebel Irhoud) around 300,000 years old, Florisbad (South Africa) about 280,000 years old, and Omo Valley (Ethiopia) about 200,000 years old. New research of the fossil record from Morocco proves the early existence of *Homo sapiens* in North Africa, which implies that our species evolved throughout the African continent.

It also proves the existence of prehistoric networks throughout Africa that early humans used. It is possible that people moved in search of food or due to climate changes. The same motives even made them move out of Africa.

Homo sapiens migrations probably happened due to rapid population growth and the search for more resources. It seems that *Homo sapiens* left Africa as early as 200,000 to 180,000 years ago, as evidenced by the fossil record found at Mount Carmel (Israel). This is important because early research on modern humans assumed they left Africa only around 100,000 to 70,000 years ago.

The emergence of *Homo sapiens* also marked the start of a very different tool production technique. Instead of large, robust tools, we see lighter, more specialized, and more sophisticated tools made of flatter stone pieces. You can read more about the stone tools made by early humans in Chapter 5.

One important feature of our species is our rapid population growth. While we do not leave as many offspring as some other species, we tend to care for our young for longer periods of time. This ensures not only the protection of our young but also encourages socialization and community building. Our strength is in our ability to group and care for one another. Prolonged childhood (which is much longer than that of other primates and even other human species) has allowed *Homo sapiens* to excel in survival and pass down important cultural practices that ensure success at hunting, using fire, building shelters, and defending each other, among other things.

Our large demographic growth also had negative consequences. More people mean more need for food and other resources. Unlike earlier human species, *Homo sapiens* put more pressure on the environment, often overhunting and using resources more rapidly. There is a marked difference in the way *Homo sapiens* and Neanderthals used natural resources. These two are very similar species biologically, but their survival strategies and culture show notable differences. We know that *Homo sapiens* likely contributed to the extinction of large predators in Europe and possibly elsewhere in the world. It is also possible that the presence of our species is linked to the disappearance of other human species, like the Neanderthals and Denisovans. Eventually, *Homo sapiens* were the only surviving hominin species on Earth.

Chapter 3 – Homo Sapiens and Neanderthals: Untangling their Relationship

For a significant duration, *Homo sapiens* and Neanderthals cohabited on the planet alongside other human species, such as the recently discovered Denisovans. How did these species interact? Did they engage in interbreeding, leaving behind traces of Neanderthal and Denisovan genes within us? And what factors contributed to the survival of *Homo sapiens* as the sole remaining human species while the others vanished from the world? This chapter serves to unravel these mysteries, providing profound insights into our ancient connections.

The Same or Different Species?

The first thing we need to cover is the question of genetic closeness between *Homo sapiens sapiens*, the Neanderthals, and the Denisovans. Were they only different variations of the same *Homo sapiens* species? Or are they close but still separate species of humans?

By estimating the gene mutation rate per generation and calibrating the data using fossil evidence, researchers can approximate the divergence times between different human species. This information helps in postulating the physical characteristics, geographic locations, and cognitive abilities of the earliest humans. It can also help scientists determine how close or distant different human groups were genetically and morphologically.

Another way to tell if two groups were the same or separate species was their ability to interbreed. This brings us to the biological species concept. According to the biological species concept, species are groups of natural populations that either currently or potentially interbreed and are reproductively isolated from other groups. The biological species concept explains that individuals belong to the same species if they can interbreed and produce fertile offspring (fertile being an important word here). We know that some close species, such as horses and donkeys, can interbreed, but they produce infertile offspring (mules). The infertility of hybrid offspring like mules highlights the challenges of gene transmission between closely related species. They cannot pass down their genes to future generations.

In the case of *Homo sapiens* and the Neanderthals and Denisovans, if these were the same species, they would be able to reproduce and leave fertile offspring, which means that today's humans would have a significant Neanderthal and Denisovan gene admixture. If this was not the case, there would be no admixture in today's human populations.

Of course, the biological species concept is more complex than this simple explanation. Species boundaries are not necessarily fixed across the entire genome, and some gene variations (alleles) can be exchanged between species. It is more accurate to consider species boundaries as semi-fixed, not completely fixed. Furthermore, it is crucial to consider that species classification is a human construct used to categorize and understand the natural world. While the distinction between species is often clear-cut in living organisms, applying this concept to extinct populations with blurred boundaries and intricate evolutionary relationships becomes more complex.

The Neanderthals and *Homo sapiens* were close species, but they show certain genetic differences that might reflect adaptations to different environments. Neanderthals inhabited regions with harsher climates, such as Europe and western Asia, potentially leading to distinct genetic adaptations. Studying these variations unveils the evolutionary dynamics that shaped *Homo sapiens* and Neanderthals.

Understanding the divergence times and the gradual emergence of anatomical features sheds light on the evolutionary history of these hominin populations. Further exploration in this domain is sure to reveal additional captivating insights into the intricate origins of humanity.

Currently, scientists have not reached a unanimous agreement on whether *Homo sapiens* and Neanderthals belonged to the same species or were separate yet closely related species. One thing is certain, though: these species interbred. Well, at least in some cases. There is Neanderthal admixture in the modern human population attesting to that.

Interbreeding between Groups

The presence of recent Neanderthal relatives among the prehistoric *Homo sapiens* indicates that interbreeding between Neanderthals and early humans was likely common in Europe. Recent advancements in genome sequencing have allowed us to extract and scrutinize Neanderthal DNA from fossil remnants, unearthing enthralling insights into the overlapping and distinctive genetic traits of these human groups. Genetic investigations provide compelling evidence of interbreeding between *Homo sapiens* and Neanderthals, which primarily occurred outside of Africa.

All of this may seem like strong proof that modern humans and the Neanderthals were the same species. However, the truth is more complex. Gene flow occurred between different hominin groups, but it was generally low, indicating that gene variations from one group were not well tolerated in the genetic background of another group. This can indicate that they were very closely related but still distinctive human groups. However, some genetic admixture survived. Modern humans are estimated to have around 1 to 4 percent Neanderthal genes (going as high as 10 percent in some human groups). This indicates that at least some Neanderthal-*Homo sapiens* offspring were fertile.

Despite the significant advancements in paleogenomics, several challenges and limitations hinder our complete understanding of Neanderthal-*Homo sapiens* interbreeding. Neanderthals and *Homo sapiens* share a remarkable number of morphological similarities, further complicating the species classification. Neanderthals possessed a similar body to modern humans. Additionally, their cranial capacity was within the range of modern humans; in fact, it was even a bit larger, suggesting comparable intellectual capabilities.

Physical similarities between *Homo sapiens* and the Neanderthals cannot always serve as solid proof of interbreeding, so we need to stick to genetics. There are similarities between the two groups that are not necessarily the product of interbreeding.

For example:

- While modern humans display similar mutations associated with red hair and pale skin, the exact mutation found in Neanderthals differs, indicating independent evolution of this phenotype in both groups.

- The advantage of reduced pigmentation in modern humans and Neanderthals living in Europe during the same period can be linked to the production of vitamin D. Paler skin allows for more efficient synthesis of vitamin D in regions with less sunlight, benefiting populations in colder climates with limited sun exposure.

- The ABO blood system gene, responsible for different blood types in humans, showed evidence that Neanderthals possibly had the O blood type. This is a blood type also found in *Homo sapiens sapiens*. However, scientists are unsure if this was a result of interbreeding (it could possibly be an independent feature).

Despite the genetic overlap and morphological similarities, proponents of the separate species classification argue that certain factors suggest reproductive isolation and distinctiveness between Neanderthals and *Homo sapiens*. Although interbreeding between Neanderthals and *Homo sapiens* occurred, evidence suggests that it was limited, possibly due to geographic and ecological barriers. This limited gene flow indicates the presence of some reproductive isolation between the two groups. Their distinct ecological adaptations and geographic distributions suggest divergent evolutionary paths and potentially support the argument for separate species classification. They may also suggest that the offspring of interbreeding was mostly infertile, which is also a sign of separate species.

So, that is one answer. The other one emphasizes similarities between these groups. We cannot deny the Neanderthal admixture in our genes; this admixture is small percentage-wise, but it exists. It is solid proof of Neanderthal-*Homo sapiens* interbreeding.

Homo sapiens and the Neanderthal Relationship

It is well known that early members of our species interacted with the Neanderthals, at least in some geographical areas. What was their relationship besides potential interbreeding? We know that these two species show a lot of similarities. Beyond genetics and morphology, investigations into cultural and behavioral aspects provide additional information about the *Homo sapiens*-Neanderthal relationship. Both groups exhibited toolmaking capabilities and control of fire and engaged in hunting and gathering. However, evidence of symbolic behaviors, such as art and personal adornments, appears more prevalent among *Homo sapiens*. These distinctions in cultural expressions raise questions about potential cognitive disparities between the two groups, which may influence their species classification.

However, artifacts discovered in Neanderthal sites demonstrate their capability for symbolic thinking and artistic expression, challenging previous assumptions about their cognitive abilities. This implies a rich cultural landscape and the potential cross-pollination of ideas and practices. They were capable of choosing appropriate wood and processing it with fire to produce tools. There are also indications of complex Neanderthal technology and advanced intelligence competency, such as the discovery of a tar-hafted flint tool. Additionally, the presence of annular (ring) constructions and traces of fire in Bruniquel Cave (France) suggests intentional construction and a level of social organization and spatial planning among Neanderthals.

It is likely that *Homo sapiens* and the Neanderthals were not so different in their behaviors as previously believed. There are some differences between the two groups, but these differences seem to be smaller than was once assumed. Their mutual encounters also do not seem to be as volatile as scientists once thought. There are more and more indications that the two groups peacefully coexisted.

The Neanderthals Go Extinct

There is also the important question of why did Neanderthals go extinct. For a long time, the explanation was that our species killed them off. Sometimes, the explanations emphasized the superiority of our species over the Neanderthals, as well as our better survival tactics. Scientists today do not believe in this theory anymore, or they propose a less extreme view of it. We know that *Homo sapiens* encountered other humans as they migrated out of Africa and that they also interbred with those groups. The extent of their interactions with other human types, like the Neanderthals, during this process, whether they displaced them or coexisted with them, remains a topic of speculation.

Insights from population genetics shed light on the dynamics between *Homo sapiens* and Neanderthals. Neanderthal populations were relatively small and geographically isolated, factors that likely contributed to their eventual extinction. In contrast, *Homo sapiens* experienced significant expansions and intermixing, potentially leading to the dilution of genetic distinctions that could support separate species designations.

Scientists highlight that fundamental ecological processes likely played a role in the Neanderthals' story. They identified competition and changes in habitat due to climate change as two key factors. Neanderthals had a relatively specialized hunting strategy focused on large Ice Age animals. However, being specialized can become a disadvantage when environmental conditions shift. With the changing climate and various animal species going extinct, the Neanderthals might have faced starvation.

An exhibit depicting Neanderthal hunters.

Some scientists emphasize the competitive advantage that *Homo sapiens* possessed over Neanderthals. While Neanderthals had physical adaptations that helped them survive in cold climates, such as large noses for warming and humidifying cold, dry air and robust bodies for conserving heat, *Homo sapiens* possessed technological innovations that Neanderthals lacked. For example, *Homo sapiens* had tools like needles for making clothing, which was crucial during the colder periods of the ice ages.

Older theories emphasized war and hostility between the *Homo sapiens* and Neanderthal populations. According to these theories, our species pushed away the Neanderthal populations from the most favorable areas. However, new findings show more evidence of coexistence between groups. This challenges the idea that Neanderthals were pushed out and disproves the forced displacement hypothesis. The discovery of stone tools, including those associated with the Mousterian culture, which was previously attributed only to modern humans, suggests peaceful interaction and possibly even tool exchange between Neanderthals and modern humans.

Contrary to popular portrayals of conflict and war between the two species, the evidence does not support the notion of a violent expulsion or a martial rivalry. The disappearance of the Neanderthals cannot be attributed to a specific epidemic or climatic catastrophe either. A possible explanation might be reproductive failure, which led to a population decline.

Complex Evolutionary Journey

The integration of Neanderthal genes into the modern human genome has unveiled the fascinating story of our ancient relatives. Unraveling the genetic parallels and disparities between *Homo sapiens* and Neanderthals illuminates a captivating narrative of our shared evolutionary journey. While both species diverged from a common ancestor, the genetic differences reflect unique adaptations to varying environments and selective pressures. The interbreeding episodes following the migration of *Homo sapiens* out of Africa further imprinted Neanderthal genetic imprints onto present-day non-African populations. Further research on this topic promises to unearth more about our ancient relatives and provide more insights into the complex mosaic of human evolution.

It is clear that the classification of these two groups is a complex endeavor. While the evidence of interbreeding aligns with the biological species concept, morphological disparities and cultural variations suggest alternative theories. The enigmatic nature of their taxonomic relationship serves as a testament to the intricate tapestry of human evolution. Further investigations, drawing upon diverse disciplines and new discoveries, will continue to refine our understanding of the captivating story woven by *Homo sapiens* and Neanderthals.

The Denisovans

The Denisovans represent an enigmatic branch in the complex tree of human evolution. They are another species closely related to *Homo sapiens sapiens* and the Neanderthals. The Denisovans are a newly discovered species. They were only identified in 2010 based on a bone fragment found in Denisova Cave in Siberia. Earlier excavations at Denisova Cave had unearthed stone artifacts believed to be of Neanderthal origin. So, when the Denisovan fossils were discovered, scientists initially assumed they were Neanderthal remains. The analyses of the DNA extracted from these fossils proved that it was a species different than the Neanderthals, although it was closely related to them. Unsurprisingly, the Denisovans, like *Homo sapiens sapiens* and the Neanderthals, come from the same archaic *Homo sapiens* origins.

As of today, researchers have identified numerous small and fragmented fossils as Denisovans based on DNA analysis. All of these fossils were found in Denisova Cave and included molars, bone chips, bone slivers, and a finger bone fragment that provided enough DNA for whole genome sequencing. Additional Denisovan fossils were discovered based on the presence of Denisovan proteins, such as a jawbone in China and a molar in Laos.

Due to the scarcity of fossil remains, our knowledge of Denisovan physical characteristics remains limited. However, recent research based on ancient DNA has provided insights into some distinctive traits. For instance, Denisovans possessed genetic adaptations related to high-altitude environments, suggesting their ability to thrive in regions with low oxygen levels, such as the Tibetan Plateau. The Denisovan genetic contributions to modern humans have been linked to several traits, including immune system responses, metabolism, and adaptation to local environments.

Physically, the Denisovans resembled Neanderthals, with their stocky build and facial features. According to present knowledge, Denisovans lived across Asia, and they came in contact with both the Neanderthals and *Homo sapiens* groups.

While our understanding of Denisovans primarily stems from genetic analyses, their cultural and technological achievements remain largely unknown. However, recent archaeological findings in Denisova Cave have provided intriguing hints about their capabilities. Artifacts, such as bone tools and jewelry, suggest that Denisovans possessed sophisticated craftsmanship skills. The discovery of stone tools in Denisova Cave suggests they had a complex culture. The artifacts, along with animal remains, indicate that the Denisovans likely hunted and consumed various animals. The stone tools resemble those found in Israel during a period of significant technological advancement (between 250,000 and 400,000 years ago).

Furthermore, the discovery of ochre markings on a bone in a Denisovan cave in Henan Province (China) provides evidence of their artistic expression and symbolic thinking. This revelation challenges the notion that cognitive abilities were limited to modern humans and Neanderthals.

A recent study revealed that the Denisovans had multiple lineages, with one closely related to the Siberian Denisovans and primarily found in East Asians and another more distantly related to the Siberian Denisovans and found in Papuans and South Asians. Present-day Papuans have a significantly greater amount of Denisovan genome fragments compared to other contemporary human populations. A third Denisovan lineage was discovered in another study, suggesting its separation from the other two around 363,000 years ago. This third Denisovan lineage was identified primarily in individuals from the island of New Guinea.

Like Neanderthals, Denisovans interbred with *Homo sapiens*, which reflects in the genes of today's humans. It is estimated that human groups with the highest Denisovan admixture (4 to 6 percent) are those in Melanesia, as well as Aboriginal groups in Australia. In contrast, mainland Asians and Native Americans have about 0.2 percent Denisovan DNA. Furthermore, a groundbreaking study unveiled evidence of interbreeding between Denisovans and Neanderthals themselves.

Contact and Interbreeding

In this chapter, we focused on the relationship between *Homo sapiens sapiens* and other closely related species. The links between these groups are complex; scientists are still trying to uncover all the aspects of interactions between *Homo sapiens*, the Neanderthals, and the Denisovans. We know that these species interacted with each other (they had to since we know they interbred), which demonstrates there was a degree of coexistence between groups, at least in specific parts of Eurasia.

How much did contact with the Neanderthals and Denisovans influence early *Homo sapiens?* The Neanderthals exhibited cultural and biological characteristics better suited for colder environments. The cultural and biological interactions between *Homo sapiens*, Denisovans, and Neanderthals likely prepared *Homo sapiens* to venture north. For example, it is possible that *Homo sapiens* migrated into Siberia and modern-day Russia before spreading into Europe.

A comprehensive picture emerges when considering genetic flow and migration patterns. As *Homo sapiens* expanded across the planet, they encountered Neanderthals and Denisovans, resulting in genetic exchanges. Europeans, who carry between 1 and 3 percent of Neanderthal genes in their DNA, are descendants of crossbreeding between *Homo sapiens* from the western Asian regions and Neanderthals. Eastern Eurasians, including various Paleo-Asian populations, were the product of crossbreeding between *Homo sapiens* who traveled eastward through the steppes (carrying Neanderthal genes) and the first Far Eastern populations, likely the Denisovans.

All these things reveal the complex relationship between different human species, but they also speak about their migration patterns. These genetic flows can help us map the migration of *Homo sapiens* out of Africa and around the globe, which we will talk about in the next chapter.

Chapter 4 – Homo Sapiens Spreads Around the World

As we detailed in previous chapters, *Homo sapiens* was not the first or only species that migrated out of Africa. Human migrations started with earlier human species, namely *Homo erectus*, around two million years ago. As it turns out, this was only the first in a series of migrations out of Africa. This was repeated with the archaic *Homo sapiens* (*Homo heidelbergensis*) around 500,000 years ago. This was how the ancestors of the Neanderthals and Denisovans found themselves in Eurasia.

However, *Homo sapiens* migrations surpassed that of earlier species. In this chapter, we will detail the journey of our species around the world. The migrations undertaken by African *Homo sapiens* are monumental events in world history. These migrations set humans apart from all other animals, as our ancestors broke free from the confines of tropical forests and adapted to diverse environments, such as the African savannahs, semidesert landscapes, Mediterranean regions, and even extreme climates like the Arctic. These remarkable adaptations primarily took place after *Homo sapiens* left Africa.

However, it is believed that Africa continuously emitted small groups of people over time, akin to a cauldron under pressure. Although this expansion out of Africa may seem gradual in human terms, it was an explosive event when considering the geological timescale. Furthermore, population movements in the opposite direction, into Africa, have also been observed, particularly in more recent millennia.

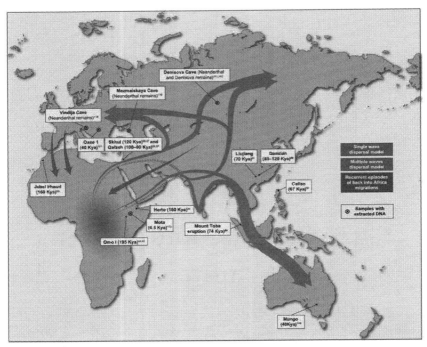

A map of migration waves in and out of Africa.
Saioa López, Lucy van Dorp and Garrett Hellenthal, CC BY 3.0
<https://creativecommons.org/licenses/by/3.0>, via Wikimedia Commons;
https://commons.wikimedia.org/wiki/File:Putative_migration_waves_out_of_Africa.png

Early Movements

Approximately two million years ago, early humans, likely *Homo erectus* or *Homo ergaster*, populated much of Africa and southern parts of Asia. Their expansion into Europe began around one million years ago, and they eventually reached the northern regions.

The migration of *Homo ergaster*, the ancestor of *Homo erectus* in Asia, represents a significant hominin movement. These species migrated northward through the arid zone that extended from the Atlantic seaboard of Africa to central Asia without encountering significant water barriers. This suggests that the notion of "getting out of Africa" may not hold true in the traditional sense, as the arid zone allowed for continuous movement without significant water obstacles. Initially coexisting with *Australopithecines* and *Homo habilis* in sub-Saharan Africa, *Homo ergaster*'s descendants spread throughout Africa and into Eurasia.

There seemed to have been numerous "waves" of migrations from Africa. An early dispersal happened around 120,000 to 100,000 years ago and stopped around 80,000 years ago. Another migration wave happened around 70,000 to 50,000 years ago. There is also a possibility of an even earlier wave, around 200,000 to 180,000 years ago.

Early modern humans also expanded to various regions in Africa itself. It is estimated that *Homo sapiens* reached western Africa around 130,000 years ago. Expansions into southern and central Africa resulted in significant divergence among human populations. There are groups within Africa today that are genetically more distant from all other groups in the world, including other Africans, as a result of early *Homo sapiens* migrations.

Migrations to Asia

The movement of the first modern *Homo sapiens* out of Africa holds significant importance. Different theories exist regarding the timing of this migration, with some placing it around 180,000 or even 200,000 years ago, while others propose a multiregional hypothesis suggesting a widespread gene exchange within a pre-modern *Homo sapiens* population. This movement occurred after the initial appearance of anatomically modern *Homo sapiens*.

These early migrations preceded the major expansion of modern *Homo sapiens* into Eurasia. Genetic evidence indicates that this route, which originated in Africa, took place between 85,000 and 55,000 years ago and likely involved maritime crossings, potentially including water routes in Southeast Asia leading to New Guinea and Australia. The possibility of crossings across the Red Sea cannot be ruled out either.

The data suggests that these migrations initially occurred in the Middle East, particularly the Arabian Peninsula. The lower sea levels and favorable climatic conditions during that time encouraged the expansion of *Homo sapiens* beyond East Africa and into Asia.

The migration model via the Bab-el-Mandeb proposes a direct route from sub-Saharan Africa, which is considered the hominin homeland, to the Middle East. However, the Bab-el-Mandeb is not the only explanation behind human expansion into Asia and the Arabian Peninsula; it is merely a possibility. It is only with the later expansion of modern *Homo sapiens* around sixty thousand years ago that a water crossing of the Red Sea aligns more closely with the genetic and archaeological evidence. This would have been part of the same migration cycle that led to the initial settlement of Australia and New Guinea, which happened approximately forty thousand years ago.

Although our understanding of the *Homo sapiens'* conquest of the north is based on limited available data, it indicates the formation of mixed populations and cultures in the Middle East, Asia Minor, and possibly further into Asia at the same latitudes. The descendants of these mixed populations, resulting from the encounter between *Homo sapiens* and Neanderthals, likely acquired survival techniques and immune systems suitable for living in the cold territories inhabited by Neanderthals.

After settling in the Levant, early humans spread through Asia. Scholars are unsure when the first groups of *Homo sapiens* reached eastern Asia, but it is highly possible that it happened during the earlier waves of migration, around 120,000 to 100,000 years ago. It is important to know that these dates are only speculation since there is not yet firm genetic evidence confirming them. A wider migration throughout Asia happened during the later migration waves.

A more recent migration wave, the one that involved the highest number of people, started around seventy-five thousand to seventy thousand years ago. These *Homo sapiens* migrated through the Middle East and into South and Southeast Asia. From there, they continued in two directions: to the north, toward China and Japan, and to the south, toward Australia and New Guinea. Scientists estimate that these *Homo sapiens* used coastal routes to move, and they reached East Asia around sixty-five thousand to sixty thousand years ago.

From there, *Homo sapiens* groups likely moved around Asia in different directions. Some of the Asian migrations were to the west. We know that human groups migrated toward the Levant and Europe, even into North and East Africa, around forty thousand years ago. This shows the complexity of *Homo sapiens* migrations—they were not exclusively happening in one direction or always toward new territories.

Finally, from East Asia, *Homo sapiens* eventually ventured farther to the east through Beringia into the Americas.

Europe

Traditionally, scientists believed that modern humans appeared in Europe around sixty thousand years ago or even later. Recently, in 2019, scientists found the remains of *Homo sapiens* in Greece that are around 200,000 years old, which is significantly older than previously thought. At the same site, anthropologists also found the remains of Neanderthals.

Europe was mostly populated during later waves of migration. The presence of *Homo sapiens* in Europe intensified around fifty thousand to forty thousand years ago. They arrived from two different directions: from the Middle East and from central Asia (a product of western migrations within Asia). This was also the time (around forty thousand years ago) that *Homo sapiens* reached northern Europe and Russia. These groups of *Homo sapiens* are the ones who encountered the Neanderthals in Europe and western Asia, interbred with them, and coexisted with them for thousands of years.

The arrival of *Homo sapiens* in Europe is marked by changes in stone tools, from typical Neanderthal tools to those linked with *Homo sapiens*. However, this explanation is often more simplified since it is possible that the Neanderthals also used those new tools. We talk more about different stone tools and traditions in the following chapter.

It has been suggested that *Homo sapiens* fully colonized Europe in fifteen thousand to twenty thousand years. This coincides with the gradual decline in the Neanderthal population, although there is still no answer as to whether *Homo sapiens* displaced them or if other factors contributed to their decline. We know that some groups of Neanderthals were displaced, probably under the populations of *Homo sapiens*. We find some of the last Neanderthal groups living in southern Europe, such as Spain, as recently as thirty thousand to twenty-five thousand years ago. The Neanderthal fossils and other traces of their presence fully disappeared around twenty-five years ago.

Australia and Oceania

Australia is one of the earliest remote areas that *Homo sapiens* populated, doing so approximately fifty thousand years ago. There are some indications that it might have happened even earlier, around sixty-five thousand years ago. This is the first example of human dispersion wider than that of *Homo erectus*.

During the Last Glacial Maximum, the sea levels were significantly lower, and a lot of Southeast Asia formed a landmass known as Sunda, while the landmass of today's Australia and New Guinea was known as Sahul. *Homo sapiens* migration crossed numerous straits between Sunda and Sahul to populate new territories.

This was a significant achievement that is still not fully understood. To reach Australia, humans had to cross wide sea channels and quickly adapt to an entirely new ecosystem upon arrival. The most plausible theory suggests that around fifty thousand years ago, *Homo sapiens* living in the Indonesian archipelago, which was separated from Asia and other islands by narrow straits, developed the first effective boats for crossing long distances over water.

To explain their progression toward Australia, it is reasonable to assume that during their time in Eurasia, *Homo sapiens* vigorously increased its population and enhanced its adaptability in the warm tropical climates to which it was already acclimated.

Populating the Americas

Most archaeologists believe that the initial settlement of the Americas occurred between twenty thousand and fifteen thousand years ago. While some researchers suggest earlier dates based on evidence at certain sites, many archaeologists argue that these claims lack the necessary cultural evidence and reliable dating methods.

The timing and routes of human migration to the Americas have been a subject of great interest. The prevailing archaeological view suggests that contemporary Indigenous peoples in the Americas have Asian ancestry. This conclusion is primarily based on biological similarities that are supported by archaeological evidence.

Initially, glaciers blocked the way from Alaska to the rest of the Americas, but around 12,000 BCE, global warming melted the ice, creating an easier passage. Taking advantage of this new corridor, humans migrated southward, spreading across the entire continent. Despite originating as Arctic hunters, they successfully adapted to a wide range of climates and ecosystems.

The prevailing theory suggests that people traveled down the coast of what is now Alaska and British Columbia in western Canada either by boat or along the coastline. This route is often referred to as the coastal migration route. Another possible entry route from Beringia was through a corridor between the two large ice sheets covering most of Canada. During periods of warming in the last ice age, the glaciers separated, creating a corridor that linked Beringia to southern areas. This route is known as the ice-free corridor route. A third possible entry route was from Europe by crossing the North Atlantic Ocean.

However, the evidence for initial entry via Beringia is much stronger, including technological and biological similarities to people from northeast Asia, as well as DNA evidence. This passageway enabled human populations to move southward, eventually reaching the central and southern parts of the Americas.

The journey to the Americas was challenging, with the first humans crossing on foot through a land bridge connecting Siberia and Alaska when sea levels were lower. This passage was even more difficult than the sea journey to Australia. The extreme Arctic conditions of northern Siberia, where temperatures could drop to minus fifty degrees Celsius and the sun rarely shone in the winter, led to *Homo sapiens* developing innovative solutions.

They learned to make snowshoes and effective thermal clothing by sewing layers of furs and skins tightly together with the help of needles. They also devised new weapons and sophisticated hunting techniques to track and kill large game, like mammoths, in the far north. With improved clothing and hunting strategies, they ventured deeper into the frozen regions, adapting their survival skills along the way. Some bands might have been driven north by wars, demographic pressures, or natural disasters, while others were enticed by the abundance of animals, such as mammoths and reindeer, in the Arctic lands.

While the ice-free corridor was a significant route, evidence suggests that *Homo sapiens* also explored and settled along the Pacific coastline of the Americas. The abundant marine resources and diverse coastal ecosystems offered new opportunities for sustenance and habitation. These coastal migrations allowed our ancestors to colonize regions like California, Oregon, and Chile, developing unique practices adapted to their coastal surroundings.

Around thirteen thousand years ago, a distinctive stone tool technology known as the Clovis culture emerged in North America. Clovis points, which are characterized by their unique shape, were used for hunting large game and became widespread across the continent. This cultural phenomenon represents a significant milestone in the Americas and offers insights into the early human presence and migration patterns there.

The prevalence of Clovis points in archaeological sites from Canada to South America indicates a significant cultural phenomenon, marking the expansion and dominance of *Homo sapiens* throughout the Americas. As more archaeological discoveries were made, it became evident that populating the Americas was not a single event or a linear migration. Instead, *Homo sapiens* likely followed multiple routes and reached different regions at varying times. For instance, evidence suggests an early presence in South America dating back over fifteen thousand years, challenging the traditional narrative of a solely northward migration.

In some sites, chipped stones resembling tools have been found, but not all archaeologists are convinced they were intentionally crafted by humans; they believe they were shaped naturally. Artifacts unquestionably made by humans exist, but doubts remain regarding their dating. Carbon-14 dating is commonly used for early sites in North America up to approximately forty thousand years ago. If a site's dating does not rely on this technique, it often faces scrutiny. Even carbon-14 dates can be disputed, particularly if there is a potential for contamination from nearby carbon-containing sediments.

One of the most groundbreaking archaeological discoveries challenging traditional migration narratives was made at Monte Verde in Chile. Excavations at this site revealed evidence of human presence dating back over fifteen thousand years ago, preceding the widely accepted Clovis culture. The Monte Verde findings, along with other pre-Clovis sites scattered across the Americas, suggest the existence of multiple migratory waves and earlier human settlements.

The Age of Migrations

Homo sapiens migrations were complex. They happened in numerous waves, so it is not possible to talk about only one migration out of Africa. These migrations went in numerous directions or back to already populated areas. Each migration wave brought new challenges and opportunities, prompting our ancestors to devise innovative solutions.

The first wave of *Homo sapiens* ventured across the Bab-el-Mandeb Strait, connecting the Horn of Africa to the Arabian Peninsula. This initial migration into Asia laid the foundation for further exploration and settlement. Our ancestors gradually populated vast regions of Asia, moving along coastlines and river valleys and eventually adapting to diverse landscapes, including deserts, forests, and mountains. The low sea levels allowed for the passage to Australia and East Asia. From East

Asia, *Homo sapiens* moved throughout the entire Asian continent. In coastal regions, the construction of boats and fishing implements facilitated the exploitation of marine resources. The development of these region-specific tools demonstrates the adaptive nature of our species.

Human arrival in Europe went from two directions: the Levant and central Asia. Upon their arrival in Europe and western Asia, *Homo sapiens* populations encountered the Neanderthal and Denisovan groups.

As the glaciers receded, our ancestors ventured into the uncharted territory of the Americas. This corridor facilitated the southward expansion of human populations, allowing them to reach the central and eventually southern parts of the Americas.

Throughout this process of expansion, *Homo sapiens* faced various challenges and exhibited remarkable adaptability. The colonization of new environments, such as the Arctic regions of Russia, required innovative strategies to overcome harsh conditions. Technological advancements, including tailored clothing, shelter construction, and food storage techniques, enabled our ancestors to thrive in these challenging environments. *Homo sapiens* adapted to diverse climates, biomes, and landscapes, significantly impacting both the environment and animal populations. Their success can be attributed to their cultural advancements and social structures.

As different groups settled in new regions, they developed distinct cultural practices, languages, art forms, and social systems. These cultural innovations were not static but instead evolved and adapted over time as they encountered new ideas and interacted with neighboring groups. We will talk about the role of language and culture for *Homo sapiens* in Chapters 6 and 7.

From its beginnings in Africa, *Homo sapiens* relied on different tools for survival. These tools provided essential assistance in activities like hunting, butchering animals, and processing plant materials. The ability to create sharp-edged tools enhanced the efficiency and success of these tasks, making it easier for early humans to acquire food and other resources necessary for survival. The next chapter focuses on stone tools humans used in prehistory.

Chapter 5 – Prehistoric Stone Tools

It is time to talk about the first human technology: stone tool production. In many ways, this is what sets the human species, including *Homo sapiens*, apart from other hominins and primates. While today's scientists believe that some animals, including primates, can and do use tools, this is generally a skill reserved for humans. This is why it's important to dedicate a chapter to prehistoric tools and how they helped early humans and *Homo sapiens* survive in different environments. Prehistoric stone tools provide invaluable insights into the lives and capabilities of our ancient human ancestors.

These tools display regional variations, reflecting the diverse cultural and environmental contexts in which they were created. Stone tool technology also played a significant role in the survival and adaptation of early humans. Tools used for hunting, gathering, and processing food allowed early humans to thrive in various environments. The development of specialized tools, such as harpoons, fish hooks, and grinding stones, further enabled the exploitation of natural resources and the establishment of settled communities.

Prehistoric stone tools can be divided into two major groups: core tools, made from the core of the stone, and flake tools, made from pieces removed from the stone. Core tools are older. Unifaces are core tools where flakes are removed from only one side. Bifaces are core tools where flakes are removed from both sides.

Classification of Prehistory

To understand the role stone tools play in human survival, it is handy to know how archaeologists and other scientists divide prehistory. These divisions depend on geography; different parts of the world have their own timelines and classifications. It is important to know this because each period and geographic location is associated with specific tool industries.

- Eurasia: Prehistoric time in Eurasia is divided into the Paleolithic period (before the invention of agriculture) and the Neolithic period (after the invention of agriculture). The Paleolithic era is divided into three distinct periods: Lower, Middle, and Upper Paleolithic. The Lower Paleolithic period is marked by the earliest stone tool industries, including the Oldowan tradition and the Acheulean tradition. The Middle Paleolithic period is notable for the emergence of Neanderthals. This period is associated with the Mousterian stone tool industry, characterized by tools such as Levallois points. The Upper Paleolithic period is characterized by *Homo sapiens* tool industries.

- Africa: The classification of prehistory in Africa is slightly different. It is divided into the Early Stone Age (from about 2.7 million years ago to about 280,000 years ago; this is the time of Oldowan and Acheulean tools), the Middle Stone Age (around 280,000 years ago to about 50,000 years ago; associated with archaic *Homo sapiens* and early *Homo sapiens sapiens*), and the Late Stone Age (appeared around fifty thousand years ago and lasted until the invention of agriculture).

- Americas: The prehistory of the Americas follows a slightly different trajectory due to the later peopling of the continent. The earliest stage characterized by stone tools is known as the Paleo-Indian period, and it lasted from the earliest arrivals of *Homo sapiens* in the Americas to about eight thousand years ago (until the domestication of plants and animals). It is best known for Clovis points that were used as arrowheads.

From the previous chapters, we know that *Homo sapiens* spread throughout the globe. It is the first human species that reached Oceania and the Americas. In Africa and Eurasia, earlier human species were present well before the appearance of *Homo sapiens*.

Before *Homo sapiens*, early humans developed their own stone tools. Typically, each human species is associated with one stone tool industry, although today, there are more and more indicators that several species used the same tools.

Early (pre-*Homo sapiens*) tool industries include:

- Oldowan tools. Present from about 1.7 to 3 million years ago. They are typically associated with *Homo habilis*.

- Acheulean tools. Present from at least 300,000 years to about 1.7 million years ago (some sources claim even to 130,000 to 150,000 years ago). Generally associated with *Homo erectus*.

- Mousterian tools. Present from about 200,000 to 300,000- years ago until 30,000 to 40,000 years ago. Mostly associated with the Neanderthals.

The Oldowan and Acheulean tools fall in the period of the Lower Paleolithic (as known in Eurasia); this was the Early Stone Age in Africa. Mousterian tools are classified as Middle Paleolithic in Eurasia and Middle Stone Age in Africa. Tools later than this are associated with *Homo sapiens* and are classified under the Upper Paleolithic (Eurasia), Late Stone Age (Africa), and Paleo-Indian period in the Americas.

Oldowan Tools

The use of stone tools dates back millions of years, with the earliest examples discovered in East Africa. The Oldowan tool industry is named after Olduvai Gorge in Tanzania, where the first significant discoveries were made by Louis Leakey in the 1930s. These simple tools were crafted by *Homo habilis* and consisted of core and flake tools, which were primarily used for cutting and scraping tasks. The Oldowan tools mark a significant milestone in human history, representing the emergence of technology and the ability to modify the natural environment for survival.

The manufacturing process of Oldowan tools involved a series of precise steps. Early hominins, likely *Homo habilis* and early *Homo erectus*, would select suitable raw materials, usually basalt or quartzite. They would then strike the rock with a hammerstone, producing sharp-edged flakes that could be used as tools. The core from which the flakes were removed was used for heavy-duty tools or as a source for future tool production.

The flakes and choppers (core tools with an irregular cutting edge) were used for various purposes, such as cutting meat, processing hides, breaking open bones to access marrow, and shaping wooden or plant materials. These tools provided early hominins with the means to exploit resources more efficiently, expanding their diet and increasing their chances of survival in a changing environment.

Oldowan chopper.
José-Manuel Benito Álvarez (España) —> Locutus Borg, CC BY-SA 2.5 <*https://creativecommons.org/licenses/by-sa/2.5*>, *via Wikimedia Commons; https://commons.wikimedia.org/wiki/File:Oldowan_tradition_chopper.jpg*

The emergence of the Oldowan tool industry suggests significant cognitive advancements in the early human species. To create and use these tools, individuals had to possess the ability to plan, conceptualize, and understand cause-and-effect relationships. The deliberate selection of suitable raw materials and the precise strikes required for flake production indicate a higher level of dexterity and mental organization compared to earlier hominins.

The production and use of Oldowan tools were not restricted to a single location or time period. Oldowan tools have been found across East Africa, including sites in Ethiopia, Kenya, and Tanzania, suggesting a widespread cultural tradition among early *Homo sapiens* populations. The consistency in tool design and production techniques across different sites indicates the transmission of knowledge and a shared cultural heritage within these ancient communities.

While the Oldowan tool industry lasted for over a million years, it was not stagnant. Archaeological evidence reveals a gradual evolution in stone tool technology, with subsequent industries, such as the Acheulean, appearing around 1.7 million years ago. The Acheulean industry, characterized by the production of hand axes and more refined bifacial tools, represented a significant advancement in stone tool technology, but it owes its existence to the Oldowan tradition.

Acheulean Tools

The Acheulean era spanned from approximately 300,000 to 1.7 million years ago. Newer research shows that it might have lasted from about 130,000 to 150,000 years ago. The Acheulean industry witnessed the development of more sophisticated stone tools. The iconic Acheulean hand ax, characterized by its teardrop shape and symmetrical design, became a hallmark of early human innovation. Hand axes were multipurpose tools used for cutting, digging, and butchering. The intricate shaping and refining of hand axes indicate a higher level of cognitive ability and planning among early humans.

An example of an Acheulean hand ax.
https://commons.wikimedia.org/wiki/File:Acheuleanhandaxes.jpg

The Acheulean industry is named after the archaeological site of Saint-Acheul in France, where the first significant discoveries were made in the mid-19th century. This tool industry is characterized by the production of distinctive handcrafted bifacial tools, including hand axes, cleavers, and picks. These tools exhibit a symmetrical shape with carefully shaped cutting edges on both sides, which were achieved through the process of flaking and shaping stones.

Who were the makers of these tools? The Acheulean tool industry is mainly associated with *Homo erectus*. The spread of these tools across Eurasia matches the spread of *Homo erectus* as a species. Today, scientists also believe that Acheulean tools were used by subsequent species, such as the archaic *Homo sapiens*, particularly *Homo heidelbergensis*.

Compared to the earlier Oldowan tools, Acheulean tools demonstrate a leap in technological sophistication. Acheulean toolmakers skillfully crafted tools by striking large flakes from a prepared core, carefully shaping them into various functional forms. The symmetrical design of Acheulean tools suggests a deliberate and planned approach to their production, which required a higher level of manual dexterity and cognitive abilities.

Acheulean tools were multifunctional and served a variety of purposes in the lives of early humans. Hand axes, the most iconic Acheulean tool, were versatile cutting and scraping implements. They could be used for butchering game, shaping wooden spears, digging, and various other tasks. Cleavers, with their sharp edges, were likely employed for heavy-duty activities like breaking bones or butchering.

The widespread distribution of Acheulean tools across Africa, Europe, and parts of Asia indicates a shared cultural tradition among *Homo erectus* and *Homo heidelbergensis* (archaic *Homo sapiens*) populations. The consistent design and manufacturing techniques suggest the transmission of knowledge, skills, and cultural practices over an extensive geographic range. Acheulean tools not only enabled survival but also fostered social cohesion and technological innovation within early human communities.

The Acheulean tool industry coincided with a time of changing climates and landscapes. The versatility and durability of Acheulean tools allowed early humans to adapt to diverse environments, from grasslands to forests and river valleys. The ability to shape their environment and exploit available resources played a crucial role in the success and survival of *Homo erectus* and early *Homo sapiens*, facilitating their expansion into new territories.

The production and use of Acheulean tools required advanced cognitive abilities. The creation of bifacial tools demanded precise planning, an understanding of the properties of raw materials, and the ability to envision the final product. The complex design and the deliberate removal of flakes from specific areas of the core suggest a high level of spatial awareness, problem-solving, and forward-thinking.

The Acheulean industry lasted for an impressive timespan, undergoing gradual but notable changes over time. Toward the end of the Acheulean period, tools became more refined, with increased symmetry and standardized shapes. This evolution eventually paved the way for subsequent industries, such as the Middle Paleolithic industries, characterized by more sophisticated tool technologies, including blades and specialized tools.

Mousterian Tools

As the human species continued to evolve, so did the complexity of stone tools. The Middle Paleolithic period, also known as the era of the Mousterian tools, saw the emergence of the Levallois technique. This technique involved carefully preparing a stone core and shaping it into various tool types by striking flakes from predetermined points.

The Mousterian industry is named after the archaeological site of Le Moustier in France, where the first significant discoveries were made in the early 20th century. This tool industry is characterized by the production of finely crafted stone tools featuring a specific technique known as Levallois flaking.

The main species associated with Mousterian tools are the Neanderthals. It is not surprising that the territory covered by the Mousterian tool industry matched the territory occupied by the Neanderthals. However, recent research points out that *Homo sapiens* have also used and produced Mousterian tools early in its existence. The Mousterian tools first appear in Europe around 160,000 years ago. Their existence in Africa and the Middle East is older, around 200,000 or even 300,000 years old. These sites are often outside of the Neanderthal geographical range, so scientists believe that our own species used Mousterian tools in these places. The Mousterian tools disappeared around thirty thousand to forty thousand years ago with the extinction of the Neanderthals.

One of the defining features of the Mousterian industry, as mentioned, is the Levallois flaking technique. This sophisticated method involved preparing a core to create predetermined shapes and sizes of flakes by removing flakes from specific points. This technique allowed toolmakers to maximize the use of raw materials and produce tools with standardized forms and sharp cutting edges.

The Levallois technique had several distinct stages. First, a core was carefully selected and prepared by shaping one or more striking platforms. Then, precise flake removals were taken from predetermined areas, usually the edges or corners of the core. These flakes were struck off in a controlled manner, using the force of a hammerstone or other striking tools. Each flake removal was predetermined, ensuring the creation of specific shapes and sizes. The Levallois technique suggests advanced cognitive capabilities among Neanderthals and early *Homo sapiens*.

Mousterian spearheads from a flint stone core.
Gary Todd, CC0, via Wikimedia Commons;
https://commons.wikimedia.org/wiki/File:Production_of_points_%26_spearheads_from_a_flint_stone_core,
Levallois_technique,_Mousterian_Culture,_Tabun_Cave,_250,000-50,000_BP_(detail).jpg

Mousterian tools were highly versatile and served a wide range of functions in the lives of Neanderthals and early *Homo sapiens*. Scrapers, with their rounded edges and sharp working surfaces, were used for tasks such as hide preparation or processing plant materials. Points, often crafted from elongated flakes or cores, were likely used as spear or arrow tips. Bifacial tools, such as hand axes and cleavers, were used for cutting, chopping, and butchering animals.

The Mousterian tool industry was not uniform. Variations in tool designs and raw material preferences can be observed across different regions and time periods. These regional differences might reflect cultural identities, population movements, or local adaptations to specific environments. The presence of Mousterian tools in regions beyond Europe, such as the Middle East and other parts of Asia, highlights the wide geographic distribution and adaptability of Mousterian technology.

The Mousterian industry witnessed gradual technological innovations over time. As populations encountered new challenges and environments, adaptations in tool design and techniques emerged. These innovations paved the way for subsequent industries, which were characterized by more sophisticated tool technologies, refined hunting strategies, and artistic expressions.

Upper Paleolithic and Late Stone Age Tools

Oldowan, Acheulean, and Mousterian tools were important for the survival of the early human species. They were essential technologies that improved the quality of life of early humans, allowing them to survive and spread throughout Eurasia. This is why Lower and Middle Paleolithic tool industries are so important for understanding the abilities and way of life of early humans.

What happened in the Upper Paleolithic (Late Stone Age) is another story. In many ways, there was a continuation of creating more efficient tools and figuring out techniques to improve them. On the other hand, with the Upper Paleolithic, we see some new trends, namely larger regional differences and specialty stone tools. Roughly, the Upper Paleolithic started around forty thousand to fifty thousand years ago and lasted until the invention of agriculture about twelve thousand years ago. Only *Homo sapiens* remained on Earth during this time, so the tools produced in this period are exclusively associated with our species.

Some scientists argue that there were early Upper Paleolithic tool industries made by the Neanderthals, such as Châtelperronian. Named after the French village of Châtelperron, these tools date from about forty thousand to forty-five thousand years ago. It is characterized by the so-called "denticulate" tools, stone tools with many edges like teeth or saws. However, some scientists do not accept the existence of this tool industry.

The Upper Paleolithic period witnessed a remarkable leap forward in tool technology. Blade technology became prevalent during this time, enabling the production of elongated, sharp-edged flakes that could be attached to handles or used as standalone tools. Other prominent tool types include burins, microliths, and projectile points. This period also saw the development of tools made from bone, antler, and ivory.

Some of the most popular Upper Paleolithic tools include:

- Blades: Blades are long, narrow flakes with parallel edges and sharp tips. They were highly versatile and served various purposes, including cutting, scraping, and engraving. Blades were often used as cores for the production of other tools.

- Burins: Burins are specialized tools with a chisel-like tip, typically used for engraving or carving materials like bone, antler, or soft stone. They allowed early humans to create intricate designs, art, and functional objects.

- Microliths: Microliths are small tools used for tasks that require high precision. They were typically used as projectile points (arrowheads). Some of these were backed tools (flakes or blades with one edge retouched to create a sharp, angled back). The retouched back enhanced the tool's stability and effectiveness. Microliths were popular tools across Africa and Eurasia during the Upper Paleolithic era.

- Projectile Points: Points and projectile points were crafted for hunting and warfare. Not all of them were microliths, and some were made of materials other than stone, such as bone or antler. These tools were designed for maximum penetration and efficiency in hunting or combat.

Tool Industries

Since there was such diversity between regions, it is not easy to classify Upper Paleolithic tool industries. We will mention only the most notable ones.

Europe

Upper Paleolithic cultures in Europe were characterized by significant advancements in tool technologies. The Aurignacian culture, one of the earliest Upper Paleolithic cultures in Europe, appeared around forty-three thousand years ago. It is associated with the development of innovative tools, such as blades made from prepared cores. These finely crafted stone tools allowed for more efficient hunting.

The Gravettian culture, which followed the Aurignacian, appeared around thirty-three thousand years ago. It is characterized by tools used in colder climates. The Gravettian culture produced many specialized tools made from bone, antler, and ivory.

The Solutrean culture followed. It appeared about twenty-two thousand years ago. It is known for its distinctive pressure flaking techniques, which allowed the development of finely crafted bifacial points. They also used projectiles (arrowheads), saws, and scrapers.

The Upper Paleolithic cultures left behind an array of magnificent cave paintings, such as those found in Lascaux and Chauvet-Pont-d'Arc in France. We will talk more about these aspects of early human culture in Chapter 7.

Asia

Asia witnessed a wide array of Upper Paleolithic cultures, each with its own unique characteristics. In the Middle East and the Levant, there was sometimes a shared tool industry with Europe. For example, there are traces of the Aurignacian culture in the Levant. During the Upper Paleolithic period in this area, microliths were extremely popular as tools.

The Ordosian culture, present in the Ordos Plateau (today's Mongolia and China), is characterized by long blades that are larger than what has been found in many other Upper Paleolithic sites. The emergence of microlithic tool industries in parts of Southeast Asia and India demonstrates the innovative ways in which these societies adapted to their environments.

Africa

As mentioned before, the African period is known as the Late Stone Age (not the Upper Paleolithic). It lasted from about fifty thousand years ago to the first use of agriculture in Africa, which happened around ten thousand years ago. Late Stone Age tools are consistent with hunting and gathering lifestyles. They often include microliths and projectile points (arrowheads). Many times, animal bones and antlers were used to create sophisticated tools.

One notable industry was the Khormusan, present in today's Egypt and Sudan. It began around forty-two thousand years ago, and it lasted until about eighteen thousand years ago. The Khormusan people displayed remarkable technological advancements by creating tools not only from stone but also from animal bones. Their culture is known for arrowheads that were precise but small in size.

The Iberomaurusian industry flourished in North Africa between around twenty-two thousand years ago and about ten thousand years ago. It was known for its microlithic tools.

The Americas: The Paleo-Indian Period

In the Americas, the first *Homo sapiens* populations developed their own stone tools and tool industries. This period, known as the Paleo-Indian period, started with the arrival of *Homo sapiens* in the Americas and lasted until the invention of agriculture about eight thousand years ago.

The most important culture of the period was the Clovis culture, named after its projectile tools (arrowheads). The culture is named after the city of Clovis in New Mexico, where stone tools were found in the early 20th century. The earliest examples of the Clovis culture date back to around fourteen thousand years ago. The Clovis culture quickly expanded across North America, leaving traces of its distinctive artifacts in various regions.

An example of a Clovis point.

This culture is characterized by projectile points for spears and arrows. These are elongated projectile points made using bifacial percussion flaking. The Clovis culture was primarily focused on big-game hunting, particularly targeting megafauna like mammoths, mastodons, and bison, which were prevalent during that time. The highly effective Clovis points enabled them to hunt these large animals with greater efficiency. Clovis hunters likely used a combination of strategies, such as cooperative hunting techniques and driving game into natural traps or narrow passes, to secure their prey.

Around ten thousand to eleven thousand years ago, Clovis points were replaced by a different type of projectile known as Folsom points. They signify the emergence of the Folsom culture throughout North America. Named after a site called Folsom in North America, these points were first described in the early 20th century. The Folsom culture was mainly present in the Great Plains in today's United States and Canada. The Folsom point is characterized by its groove that runs almost the entire length of the projectile point. This allowed for a tighter grip between the projectile point and its wooden base (spear or arrow). Anthropologists also discovered that some Folsom points were used as knives.

Both the Clovis and Folsom cultures are important for understanding the presence of early *Homo sapiens* in the Americas. They challenged the prevailing understanding of how the Americas were populated and highlighted the ingenuity and resourcefulness of early human populations. Archaeological evidence has fueled ongoing debates and research regarding the timing, routes, and patterns of human migration into the Americas.

Homo sapiens' Tool Use

As *Homo sapiens* migrated to different regions with distinct ecological settings, they encountered diverse landscapes and resources. This led to the development of specialized stone tools tailored to specific environments. Different regions developed unique tool industries with specific manufacturing techniques, raw material preferences, and stylistic features. This cultural diversity emphasizes the dynamic nature of early human societies and the significance of local environmental conditions and cultural interactions.

For example, in areas where large game was abundant, the invention of spear points and projectile weapons, such as the Clovis points in North America or the Solutrean points in Europe, facilitated effective hunting and improved the chances of securing food. These finely crafted tools allowed for long-range hunting, enabling early humans to take down larger and more formidable prey.

A comparison between a six-foot human and an American mastodon.
Dantheman9758 at en.wikipedia, CC BY 3.0 <https://creativecommons.org/licenses/by/3.0>, via Wikimedia Commons; https://commons.wikimedia.org/wiki/File:High_res_mastodon_rendering.jpg

In coastal regions, where marine resources were abundant, specialized stone tools were developed to aid in fishing and shellfish gathering. For instance, the creation of fish hooks, harpoons, and shellfish-processing tools like shell scrapers and drills enabled *Homo sapiens* to exploit coastal resources more efficiently. These tools played a crucial role in expanding the diet and subsistence strategies of early humans, facilitating their migration and settlement along coastlines.

In addition to hunting and gathering, the development of stone tools for woodworking and construction played a vital role in human migration. Tools like adzes, axes, and scrapers allowed early humans to shape wood for building shelters and crafting boats. Moreover, the invention of smaller, more delicate stone tools, such as scrapers, burins, and blades, marked the transition to more intricate and versatile toolkits during the Upper Paleolithic period. These tools allowed for more refined and specialized tasks, including detailed crafting, hide processing, and the creation of composite tools like spears with stone tips.

The invention and refinement of stone tools not only facilitated survival but also shaped the cultural and social dynamics of our ancestors, playing a pivotal role in human migration and the colonization of the world.

Chapter 6 – Human Cognition and Language

Tool use among early human species and *Homo sapiens* shows they had cognitive abilities. The development of human cognition is an important topic for human evolution. The increase in brain size, physical changes in the body, tool use, and the development of language—all these things speak of remarkable cognitive changes in humans compared to other animals.

Great apes demonstrate certain cognitive and empathic abilities. Chimpanzees, for example, are capable of toolmaking and tool usage for acquiring food and social displays. They employ moderately complex hunting strategies that require cooperation, and they recognize a social hierarchy. They can even learn to use symbols. However, the abilities of early humans, particularly *Homo sapiens*, were remarkably different.

The Emergence of Human Intelligence

The question of human intelligence and how it evolved is still not completely solved. Different scientists have offered numerous ideas on how it might have developed. We know that the increased intelligence of early humans played a key role in acquiring food through the use of tool technology. This is why tool use is so important in figuring out the evolution of human cognition since few other traces of early human life are left.

The transformation of the hand during hominin evolution helped greatly. The hand serves as a way to dole out information and communicate with others. It also helps to build tools more easily.

In the past, archaeologists tended to view stone tools as physical products resulting from cognitive activities occurring within hominin brains. A more recent approach considers stone tools as sources of insight into hominin cognition and recognizes their role in the development of human thought and intelligence.

Other theories emphasize the role of socialization in the development of human cognition. Some studies propose that social exchange might have played a crucial role. This adaptation is believed to have evolved with early humans. With the advancement of complex social structures among humans, social skills became invaluable for survival. Also, the ability to communicate complex concepts through language patterns became increasingly crucial. Consequently, individuals who were more socially adept and communicative gained an advantage over others.

Humans, among other species, possess cognitive and mental capacities to establish extensive personal relationships and connections. These concepts suggest that human cognitive complexity arose from the increased social complexity of living in larger groups. These larger groups brought about a greater number of social relationships and interactions, thereby promoting increased intelligence in early humans.

Some scientists propose that human intelligence evolved as a result of sexual selection rather than survival needs. According to this view, intelligence might have served as an indicator of healthy genes.

There is still no consensus on what drove the rapid development of intelligence among early humans. It was likely a result of several factors. Interestingly, an older popular theory about human cognition is now mostly abandoned. This theory proposed that human cognition and intelligence are a product of increased meat consumption dating back to *Homo erectus*. While there might be some truth to it, scientists cannot find direct evidence linking nutrition to the evolution of intelligence.

What we do know is that there are numerous advantages of intelligence for a group, such as language, communication, teaching, and cooperation. All of these contribute to a group's survival potential. Humans are social beings, and these traits are believed to have existed back with early humans before *Homo sapiens*. Thus, it is possible that human cognition is strongly linked to group survival and cooperation.

Physical Changes and Cognition

The development of human cognition happened concurrently with the development of specific physical changes. In many ways, these physical changes during hominin evolution led to the development of cognition; likewise, the development of larger brains and human cognition caused certain physical changes in early humans.

The first thing that needs to be emphasized is the emergence of bipedalism. As noted in earlier chapters, walking upright was the first notable aspect of hominin evolution that set early hominins apart from apes.

Bipedalism served as the foundation for the evolution of the hand and various other transformative changes in the human body. Bipedalism freed hands, which allowed hominins to move in a more efficient way, and it also opened up the possibility of toolmaking and tool use. By freeing the upper limbs, bipedalism enabled early humans to take on new tasks and reshaped the entire body.

A larger brain necessitated a larger skull and was accompanied by other morphological and biological changes. One such change was the widening of the birth canal to accommodate the larger skulls of newborns. This adaptation led to early childbirth, before the skull grew too large to pass through the birth canal. This adaptation allowed the human brain to continue growing but imposed new constraints. For instance, human infants are born with a skull and brain that are still unfinished and remarkably immature compared to other animal species. After birth, the human brain continues to rapidly grow in size. During this time, the child is unable to care for itself, so it depends on the care of others in the group.

Beginning with *Homo ergaster*, brain growth occurred at the cost of relative muscle power. Humans are physically weaker than great apes. Another important change was the shortening of the intestines. Apes possess large intestines suitable for processing food that is not rich in nutrients, such as leaves and other plant food. This is not true for the human species. The shortening of the intestines was apparent in *Homo ergaster*, who had a diverse diet consisting of both plant material and some meat (particularly fish). Later species of humans relied even more on meat, which reflected in the further shortening of the intestines. These changes made a huge impact on human nutrition and the type of food we use for necessary nutrients and energy.

Human vs. Animal Communication

Another crucial aspect of *Homo sapiens* cognition is the development of language. Human language abilities are different from animal communication. Human language relies on symbols, which allows our species to express complex thoughts, ideas, and behaviors.

While animals rely on signals that pertain to their immediate surroundings, human language extends far beyond the present moment. Language encompasses our inner world of thoughts, memories, plans, fantasies, and dreams, providing us with a remarkable tool to communicate. This has played a significant role in our success as *Homo sapiens*.

Numerous animal species employ complex systems of signals for communication. However, there is a crucial distinction between animal signals and human language. Animal signals solely relate to the immediate environment, while human language enables communication about abstract concepts, distant realities, and even nonexistent phenomena.

There are notable anatomical distinctions between apes and humans that allow for the development of language. One significant difference is that human brains are much larger than that of apes, particularly in the frontal lobe. Specific brain areas have adapted to handle a language with an extensive vocabulary. While no regions of the brain are exclusively dedicated to language, the areas most closely associated with language are Wernicke's area, where the analysis of incoming sounds occurs, and Broca's area, which is responsible for speech production.

This anatomical change is believed to be a primary factor in the development of speech about 250,000 years ago. This was around the time when the early *Homo sapiens* emerged, although we cannot be sure which human species was the first to use spoken language. It is probable that the archaic *Homo sapiens* used some form of language, including some form of speech.

Homo sapiens possess a unique ability to construct a vast array of sounds using a limited number of sounds. This is due to our vocal apparatus. Breathing also plays an important role. To maintain continuous speech, it is crucial to have voluntary control over one's breathing. Studies among apes and humans show that humans exhibit much greater voluntary control over their breathing.

Anatomically, the descended larynx helps humans produce precise sounds that are used in language, which is yet another change acquired during evolution. However, the descended larynx also presents a disadvantage, as it increases the risk of choking on food that enters the windpipe. Unlike other apes, humans cannot swallow and breathe simultaneously. This means that the evolutionary benefits of spoken language must be so important that they compensate for such a large disadvantage.

Another anatomical difference between humans and apes is that the nerve fibers in the spinal column responsible for chest movements are thicker in humans than in chimpanzees. We know that *Homo erectus* had a relatively thin nerve channel, similar to chimpanzees. This might suggest that *Homo erectus* had not yet gained full control over its vocal apparatus.

Language Development

The emergence of language remains an enigma in human evolution. The debate on the origins of language remains unsettled, with various theories proposing different explanations. Did language emerge with the Neanderthals (or even earlier) or with fully modern humans? Interestingly, the brain functions required for tool production across generations are consistent with those needed for language production.

Bipedalism freed our hands, allowing us to engage in complex actions, and hands became one of the earliest forms of communication. Hand gestures and other physical ways to communicate eventually led to the emergence of language. Even today, hand gestures continue to complement spoken language, as we naturally use our hands to emphasize and reinforce what we are talking about. The range of meanings conveyed through hand movements is extensive, and they often mirror the characteristics of spoken language.

The use of hands, the body, and the voice to communicate is present among all great apes. This form of communication began with body language and facial expressions and gradually expanded to include hand gestures and vocalizations among early humans. Over time, the introduction of articulate sounds led to the formation of spoken words and verbal language.

Some scientists propose that the primary driving force behind the development of language was the need to maintain larger social groups.

The transition to life in the savannah presented significant challenges to hominids, as they became more vulnerable to predators in open spaces. To protect themselves, they were compelled to form larger groups. However, internal conflicts are more likely to arise in larger groups. Chimpanzees live in bands of approximately 50 individuals, while early human groups consisted of about 150 to 200 members. This meant it would have been more challenging to maintain cohesion among human groups compared to chimpanzee ones. Language might have been a way to communicate more efficiently and keep social cohesion.

Prior to the development of language, early hominids communicated through gestures. Language, therefore, is a relatively recent development in human existence. Most elements of human cognition had already evolved long before the advent of language.

Protolanguage

The transition from gestural communication to a fully developed language with grammar likely involved several stages. There is a proposed simplified "protolanguage" of early humans. Scientists believe that this development is reflected in the language acquisition of children. For example, toddlers begin by using simple words and later move to simple two-word sentences before gradually acquiring mastery over their native language.

Scientists suggest that *Homo erectus* mastered this protolanguage and that it was not until *Homo sapiens* that a language with grammatical structure emerged. This viewpoint aligns with other scientific assumptions that *Homo erectus* communicated through gesturing with some vocalizations.

Homo heidelbergensis is thought to have made controlled vocalizations and perhaps even developed an early form of symbolic language.

Recent studies indicate that the Neanderthals might have possessed a language more advanced than protolanguage but not as complex as *Homo sapiens* language. Both species engaged in spoken language and used symbols in ornaments and paintings.

The discourse surrounding Neanderthal language largely revolves around whether they possessed the ability to vocalize in a manner similar to modern humans. Unfortunately, the lack of direct evidence pertaining to their throat length, tongue structure, or palate prevents us from forming any conclusions. Regardless of their vocal capabilities, it is probable that the Neanderthals communicated through an array of actions and sounds.

Human Language and Cognition

The development of human cognition, intelligence, and language are important milestones in the evolution of *Homo sapiens*. While we are still not sure how these steps occurred, we know that the evolutionary changes in the brain correlated with changes in the physical body. The development of human cognition allowed early humans to form strong social groups and master toolmaking, all of which helped with survival.

Furthermore, language development among early humans made for more effective and richer communication. Language creation and utilization are inherent to all human beings, serving as universal traits that unite us and facilitate cross-cultural communication, despite the immense diversity of cultural experiences across the globe. It is now time to turn to these cultural experiences and their importance for early human and *Homo sapiens* communities.

Chapter 7 – Homo Sapiens Paleolithic Culture

Culture has played a crucial role in promoting social cooperation and fostering cohesive group dynamics among early *Homo sapiens* groups. Cooperation and group cohesion have been vital for human survival, enabling collective action in tasks such as hunting, gathering, defense, and resource management.

Culture has also provided humans with flexibility, allowing for rapid adaptation to changing circumstances. Unlike genetically determined behaviors seen in other species, human culture allows for the modification and adaptation of behaviors in response to new challenges. This has proved critical in humans' ability to occupy diverse ecological niches and colonize different environments across the globe. Culture and biology are intricately intertwined, coevolving and influencing each other throughout human evolution. In other words, cultural practices have shaped our biological traits and vice versa.

The transmission of knowledge through cultural practices allows for the preservation and refinement of complex skills and techniques. For example, early humans passed down hunting strategies, toolmaking techniques, and medicinal plant knowledge through oral traditions.

We already talked about an important aspect of early human culture in Chapter 5: toolmaking. In Chapter 6, we mentioned another important aspect of culture: language, its origins, and its importance for *Homo sapiens* as a species. It is now time to take a look at other aspects of early *Homo sapiens* culture during the Paleolithic period before the invention of agriculture.

Hunting, Gathering, and Control of Fire

For the longest time, humans were hunters and gatherers. Obtaining food required physical prowess, keen observation skills, and strategic thinking. Archaeological evidence supports the idea that hunting developed gradually alongside other forms of resource collection. Foraging and opportunistic scavenging likely played significant roles before hunting became a regular occurrence. The establishment of hunting as a significant activity coincided with the evolution of bipedalism. *Homo ergaster* and *Homo erectus*, who had bodily proportions similar to ours, represent the first human species in which hunting behaviors likely emerged.

Hunting strategies varied depending on the prey and the environment. Persistence hunting, for example, involved tracking and chasing animals over long distances until they succumbed to exhaustion. Cooperative hunting involved coordinated efforts of multiple individuals to surround and capture larger game. The success of a hunt depended on factors like tracking animals, developing effective hunting techniques, and utilizing appropriate tools and weapons. Gathering strategies focused on identifying and harvesting edible plants, fruits, nuts, and roots. In prehistory, hunting and gathering were a way of life that shaped early human existence. They provided sustenance, challenges, and opportunities for cultural expression and social organization.

Mastery over fire is one of the most pivotal moments in prehistory. Our ancestors discovered the transformative power of fire, first accidentally and then intentionally through the controlled use of fire. Cooking became a crucial practice that greatly improved the utilization of food resources.

In Africa, scientists have uncovered traces of fire dating back at least 1.5 million years. In Europe, *Homo heidelbergensis* mastered fire around 700,000 years ago. The origin of fire utilization can be traced through the discoveries of ancient hearths, some dating almost 800,000 years ago.

Fire provided an advantage to early humans, who consumed as much animal protein as possible. Additionally, mastering fire had practical applications, as seen in *Homo heidelbergensis* sites, where wood spears were burned to increase their hardness, showcasing the early use of fire for purposes other than cooking.

Some scientists argue that fire is linked to the rapid development of the brain between 1.6 and 1.8 million years ago in *Homo ergaster* in Africa and *Homo erectus* in Asia. This connection is attributed to the advantage gained by humans who consumed animal protein extensively. However, there is still no definite proof that food intake, particularly meat, prompted rapid brain development in early humans.

In the Paleolithic era, fire was extremely important, especially during the Ice Age. The most recent ice age, which covered broad areas of Europe, Asia, and North America in heavy blankets of ice, lasted from roughly 100,000 to 8000 BCE. As sea levels dropped, previously nonexistent land bridges emerged, enabling human migration.

The Ice Age presented a significant threat to human existence, necessitating the ability to adapt for survival. Notably, early humans demonstrated their adaptability by altering the environment rather than solely adjusting themselves to better suit their surroundings. The utilization of fire serves as a reminder of their adaptive strategies.

Social Organization

Hunter-gatherers were the earliest social framework. Groups of early humans roamed nature, gathering plants, hunting animals, and probably scavenging when the chance arose. These small bands moved in isolation from other human groups, but they fostered cooperation between members of the group. This cooperation was crucial for ensuring the survival and protection of all individuals. It also facilitated the transmission of valuable knowledge across generations.

A typical early human group consisted of a small band of up to one hundred individuals, although fifty to seventy-five was the norm. Most of the time, these individuals were related to each other, such as parents, children, and grandparents. However, some bands also included several family groups or individuals not related to each other.

The main role of these social groups was to ensure survival. This meant fulfilling basic biological needs: food, shelter, protection, and reproduction. The main way to ensure this was a strong sense of group belonging and heightened social bonds.

Early groups of *Homo sapiens* and other human species were highly social beings. Their sense of belonging to a group was strong. A band of fifty people could survive in the wild, but an individual could not survive on their own. *Homo sapiens* remarkable empathetic abilities and strong drive to belong explain modern humans' tendency to protect the vulnerable.

However, altruism among early humans cannot be explained solely by practical motivations. There is proof that the Neanderthals and early *Homo sapiens* cared for the sick and injured individuals in their groups. It is not impossible that some of this altruism dates back to the earliest humans, such as *Homo erectus*, or even earlier to other primate groups.

In addition to social bonds and altruism, early human groups ensured survival through careful organization of tasks. The division of labor was typically done by gender. In hunter-gatherer groups, men were typically responsible for hunting and fishing, while women were in charge of gathering berries and other plant food. However, this was not an absolute rule: there is proof that women were hunters in many *Homo sapiens* communities.

Over time, *Homo sapiens* transitioned from living in small groups dependent on nature to increasingly larger and more organized groups, where individuals had to adhere to social rules to secure necessary resources for survival. Small bands of individuals eventually joined each other, creating larger groups that shared a common culture. These larger groups, known as tribes, consisted of several family groups or clans. Forming larger groups made sense. Large hunting teams could be more successful than smaller ones, and larger groups could provide more socialization for their members, providing better protection.

Artistic Expression

Hunting and gathering societies developed rich cultural traditions that included art, music, storytelling, rituals, and spiritual beliefs. These cultural expressions served as a means of communication and social cohesion.

Cave paintings, rock art, and engraved objects provide invaluable insights into the artistic expressions of early hunting and gathering communities. These works depict hunting scenes, animals, and symbols that held cultural and symbolic significance. They reflect the deep reverence that early humans had for the natural world and their close connection with it.

Artistic and spiritual expression is very old and can be traced to early humans, even before the emergence of *Homo sapiens*. The most impressive and best-preserved examples of prehistoric art are cave paintings. They started to appear around forty thousand years ago and were found throughout the world. However, the most famous examples are cave paintings from France and Spain, such as Chauvet Cave and Lascaux (France) and Altamira and the Cave of El Castillo (Spain). The paintings often display a deep understanding of the animals they depict, capturing their physical attributes and movements with great precision.

A cave painting found in Lascaux.
https://commons.wikimedia.org/wiki/File:Lascaux_painting.jpg

The purpose of cave paintings remains a subject of ongoing debate among scholars. Some theories propose these artworks served ritual or ceremonial purposes, possibly related to hunting practices or shamanistic beliefs. Others suggest they acted as visual narratives, conveying stories or myths within early human communities. Regardless of their exact purpose, cave paintings provide valuable insights into the cultural practices and artistic sensibilities of early humans.

Prehistoric art is also characterized by figurines made of stone, antler, bone, wood, and other materials. Many represent female figures, although animals and abstract figurines are also present. Perhaps the most famous example of this artistic expression is the Venus of Willendorf, discovered in the early 20th century in Austria. This figurine of a voluptuous naked woman is about twenty-five thousand to thirty thousand years old. It is the most popular example of the so-called "Venus figurines" that were popular in prehistory.

Venus of Willendorf.
User:MatthiasKabel, CC BY-SA 3.0 <http://creativecommons.org/licenses/by-sa/3.0/>, via Wikimedia Commons; https://commons.wikimedia.org/wiki/File:Venus_von_Willendorf_01.jpg

What was the purpose of these figurines? Some might have served as objects of veneration or religious significance, representing deities or supernatural beings within the belief systems of ancient cultures. Others might have been utilized for practical purposes, such as fertility symbols or tools for magical or healing rituals. The wide range of subject matter and styles seen in prehistoric art reflects the diverse cultural and spiritual beliefs of early human societies.

Artistic expression of early *Homo sapiens* groups can also be seen in adornments, such as pearls, shells, stones, antlers, and teeth. These were worn individually or as part of clothing. Some of these adornments could have served as a marker of clans or another type of social belonging.

Spiritual Beliefs

It is difficult to understand the spiritual beliefs of the earliest humans. We know that early *Homo sapiens* groups took special care when burying their dead, and there are potential indicators of rituals surrounding the burials that speak about early humans' spiritual beliefs. Grave goods (objects buried with the deceased) were common in Paleolithic burials. These items included tools, weapons, jewelry, and personal belongings. The inclusion of grave goods suggests early humans believed the deceased would require these possessions in the afterlife or that they held symbolic significance in facilitating the transition to the spiritual realm.

Another notable aspect of Paleolithic burials is the presence of deliberate burial sites. These sites were often located in caves, rock shelters, or other specific areas. The choice of burial location was likely influenced by a spiritual connection to the natural environment or a belief in sacred spaces. These burial sites might have served as places of reverence where the living could connect with the spirits of the departed.

The positioning and treatment of the bodies within the burial sites also indicate ritualistic practices. Paleolithic humans sometimes buried their dead in a flexed position, suggesting symbolic gestures associated with birth or rebirth. Additionally, the bodies were sometimes adorned with pigments or ochre, indicating a belief in the power of these substances to aid in the transition to the afterlife or signifying spiritual transformation.

Paleolithic burials were not limited to humans alone. The remains of animals, including those hunted for sustenance, have been found alongside human burials. This practice suggests a belief in the spiritual significance of animals and their role in the afterlife or as companions to the deceased.

Gender in Prehistory

The role of women in Upper Paleolithic societies remains largely mysterious, despite the abundance of female figurines found in archaeological sites. Hunting and gathering societies generally had a division of labor based on gender roles, although we know that it wasn't always strict. There were many women hunters in Paleolithic communities. The production and use of specific tools might have been associated with distinct gender roles or activities. The distribution of these tools within archaeological sites may offer clues about the involvement of men and women in various tasks.

Understanding gender in prehistory requires exploring social organization and power dynamics within ancient societies. Factors such as kinship, age, social status, and individual agency likely influenced the distribution of power and authority in these communities. Piecing together these elements can help us form a more comprehensive understanding of gender dynamics in prehistoric societies.

Moving toward Sedentarism

Social dynamics within Paleolithic cultures varied depending on the region and available resources. These societies were generally egalitarian, with relatively small groups composed of extended families or bands. Cooperation and sharing played a crucial role in their survival. Resources, including food and tools, were often shared within the group, ensuring everyone's well-being. Gender roles were likely flexible, with both men and women contributing to hunting and gathering. The absence of permanent settlements and the constant need to move made social relationships crucial for the survival and success of these communities.

In Paleolithic times, *Homo sapiens* was a nomadic species with no permanent settlements. This was required by the hunting and gathering lifestyle: people had to move with the animals and seek places with plant food. This lifestyle was practiced for centuries.

However, around 10,000 BCE, things started to change. There was a marked shift in subsistence strategies and lifestyle. After thousands of years of hunting and gathering, humans started to build permanent settlements. Even more importantly, *Homo sapiens* invented a different approach to subsistence: agriculture. This created a crucial turning point in the evolution of our species. In the following chapter, we'll go into greater detail on how domesticating plants and animals has benefited *Homo sapiens*.

Chapter 8 – The Invention of Agriculture

Around eleven thousand to twelve thousand years ago, humans made a pivotal change in their subsistence strategies by domesticating plants and animals. This had a profound effect on the lives of *Homo sapiens*. With the advent of agriculture, humans started to produce their own food and also began to build permanent settlements (farming villages). Early farmers selected varieties of plants that had traits suitable for mature harvesting, resulting in increased yields over time.

In this chapter, we will discuss the most important aspects of Neolithic times: the invention of agriculture, plant and animal domestication, and the switch to permanent settlements.

The term "Neolithic" was originally coined by Sir John Lubbock in the mid-19th century. Later, V. Gordon Childe coined the term "Neolithic Revolution" to describe significant changes in *Homo sapiens* communities that began with the introduction of agriculture, particularly a switch from food foraging (hunting and gathering) to food production (farming), as well as a switch from nomadic lifestyles to permanent settlements.

Today, scientists are a bit critical of the term "Neolithic Revolution" because it implies rapid and complete changes. In reality, the switch to plant and animal domestication was a gradual process that took thousands of years, starting with the domestication of the wolf (turning the animals into what we know as domesticated dogs today) around twenty thousand years ago. It also included the gradual stockpiling of wild grasses and other plants. Also, not all human communities switched to agriculture in prehistory. There are still hunting and gathering groups who practice nomadic lifestyles in the world today.

Early domestication of plants and animals has been recorded in various regions, primarily in southwestern Asia (the Levant, Turkey, and Iraq). These places provide evidence of early agriculture with wheat and barley cultivation, as well as the domestication of sheep and goats. Scientists believe that plant and animal domestication spread from these places throughout Eurasia and Africa. However, we also know that some places invented plant and animal domestication on their own, such as regions in Africa. Scientists also believe this was what happened in the Americas, where agriculture was independently invented around 8000 BCE.

These two pivotal developments—crop cultivation and animal domestication—enabled humans to break free from a nomadic lifestyle centered on searching for sustenance.

Domesticating Plants and Animals

The process of domestication involves two steps: cultivation and selection. Cultivation refers to the choosing and management of wild plants or animals, while selection involves the reproduction of specific variants to better suit human needs.

Plant and animal domestication was a gradual process that happened over many centuries. It started with the domestication of the first animal—the wolf—at least twenty thousand years ago, if not earlier. This was also a gradual process that began with hunting and gathering communities probably as early as thirty thousand years ago.

Dogs initially formed a partnership with humans in hunting activities. The first signs of dog domestication are found in graves containing human skeletons and dog remains. It is believed that wolves initially interacted with humans near hunter-gatherer camps, as they were attracted by the food waste. Humans recognized the benefits of keeping wolves as companions, guard dogs, and scavengers. Through selective breeding, a mutually beneficial relationship between humans and dogs developed, leading to the domestication of these animals. The process of domestication involved genetic changes in wolves to transform them into dogs, including reduced skull size, reduced fur length, modified ear shape, and more. Also, humans selectively bred wolves for reduced aggression, favoring more docile animals.

When it came to plants, early domestication likely started with stockpiling plants suitable for human consumption. First, hunter-gatherers collected favorable plant food and burned unfavorable ones in the soil, probably to encourage certain wild plants to grow. Over time, humans continued to cultivate wild plants with deliberate planting and sowing. It is possible that at this stage, humans also selected specific plants with desirable traits to grow and stored some seeds for future use.

The deliberate selection of plants led to changes in plant morphology, altering wild plants into domesticated ones. Early farmers selected and cultivated varieties that had traits favorable for farming. The earliest domesticated plants were wheat, barley, and rice. In the Americas, humans domesticated corn.

As a result of selective breeding, many crop plants have undergone significant changes from their wild counterparts. They exhibit specific characteristics, such as larger size, bigger fruits and seeds, and hardiness. These changes have been essential in the development of agriculture and have shaped our present-day crops.

Domesticated plants have higher seed yields than wild ones, which means they produce more food. They require a specific amount of land to grow, which led to the first farms. Farming required people to tend to the land, which, in turn, resulted in the first permanent settlements. At the same time, the surplus food allowed for a larger population, which led to groups increasing in size.

Early farmers cleared land, prepared fields, and engaged in sowing and harvesting. They learned to control water resources through irrigation systems, ensuring optimal conditions for plant growth. With time, farmers developed knowledge of crop rotation, allowing them to maintain soil fertility and maximize agricultural productivity.

The practice of domesticating animals emerged alongside farming. Early humans recognized the benefits of keeping animals close to their settlements. They began to tame and breed certain wild animals for various purposes. Animal domestication provided a sustainable source of sustenance, such as meat, milk, and eggs. It also provided vital resources for clothing, housing, and tools, such as wool, hides, and bones. Furthermore, the bond between humans and tamed animals extended beyond utilitarian needs. Animals also held cultural and symbolic significance. They were integrated into religious rituals, artwork, and mythologies.

People experimented with local animals to determine which species were suitable for domestication and provided desirable food sources. Creating suitable environments to attract and control animals was a crucial aspect of domestication. These environmental modifications ranged from protecting animals from predators to providing them with food and water and closely monitoring them throughout their life cycles.

All these changes led to the concentration of people, plants, and animals near water resources, such as rivers and oases, fostering new relationships of dependence between humans, plants, and animals and ultimately resulting in domestication.

Notable Sites

The earliest traces of Neolithic changes were found in the Fertile Crescent, a wide area in southwestern Asia stretching from the Mediterranean to today's Iraq. Throughout western Asia, there are numerous sites that showcase settled communities of farmers. Neolithic farming began with people gathering wild plants, such as barley and wheat; from these beginnings, communities slowly started to cultivate their own grains. Many of these places also started to domesticate animals but often at a later date.

Here are some notable early Neolithic sites from the Middle East:

- Jericho (the Jordan Valley). Known for early domestication of grains like wheat and barley. Proof of plant domestication dates back to around 8300 BCE. Jericho was one of the earliest examples of large farming villages in the world. It is also notable for a stone wall that encircled the village, which is one of the earliest examples of fortification.

- Jarmo (today's Iraq). The site dates back to approximately 7000 BCE. The houses at Jarmo were constructed using pressed mud, with later structures featuring stone foundations. Houses had ovens built in the floor. We know that people at Jarmo grew barley and wheat, and there are also traces of domesticated animals (sheep and goats).

- Catal Huyuk (today's Turkey). Dates back to between 7400 and 6000 BCE. Despite its late emergence, Catal Huyuk boasted an exceptionally dense population. This site is characterized by mud houses with an entry through the roof.

These Neolithic sites from the Middle East provide valuable insights into the early stages of agricultural development. They show the transition from a nomadic lifestyle to settled farming communities, where crop cultivation formed the foundation of human sustenance and progress. The practices and innovations pioneered at these sites laid the groundwork for the advancements and civilizations that would follow.

Pottery

Another significant Neolithic change is the invention of pottery. Large quantities of grain needed suitable vessels for storing, which prompted people to shape clay and other materials, leading to the development of pottery. This was also a gradual process that began even before Neolithic times. We know that some hunting and gathering groups developed pottery as early as twenty thousand years ago, if not earlier.

Pottery is very useful as a container, as it can also be used to store liquids. However, pottery has its disadvantages: it is bulky, heavy, and fragile. It was not practical for mobile foraging lifestyles, so it became more prevalent once people started to settle down during Neolithic times. From a practical standpoint, pottery vessels enabled the storage, transportation, and preparation of food, leading to improved nutrition and culinary practices. Decorative techniques, such as painting, carving, and glazing, embellished pottery vessels with intricate patterns, symbols, and narratives. These designs not only added aesthetic value but also conveyed cultural identities, religious beliefs, and historical events.

Examples of ancient pottery from Mesopotamia.
Daderot, CC0, via Wikimedia Commons; https://commons.wikimedia.org/wiki/File:Samarra_pottery_-_Oriental_Institute_Museum,_University_of_Chicago_-_DSC06931.JPG

While pottery and agriculture are not always directly related, we can say that they are closely linked. Archaeologists consider pottery a notable aspect of Neolithic cultures. The wheel was initially invented for pottery production around 5,500 years ago in Mesopotamia and later adapted for transportation. This technological advancement resulted in the production of pottery on a much larger scale. The wheel itself consisted of a rotating platform powered by human force. The potter would sit or stand beside the wheel and use their hands to shape the clay as it spun. This technique provided greater control over the vessel's symmetry and thickness, resulting in more consistent and refined pottery.

Sedentarism and Surpluses

Instead of wandering in pursuit of food sources, people began to settle down to cultivate crops on a regular basis. This shift facilitated the sustenance of larger populations and led to the development of villages, which gradually transformed into organized societies. Within these communities, people began storing food and engaging in trade.

The Neolithic time brought demographic changes to early societies. As humans settled in one place, they were able to have more children, leading to the expansion of families. The advent of agriculture brought about a surplus of food and resources that allowed for the support of larger populations. It also enabled others to pursue occupations and leisure activities beyond food production.

Life in these societies was comparatively easier than in agricultural societies where populations were smaller. However, the larger the society, the more labor is required to provide food for the people.

As societies transitioned to a sedentary lifestyle, permanent structures, such as houses, granaries, and storage facilities, were constructed. The shift from temporary shelters to durable dwellings allowed for the accumulation and preservation of surplus food and resources. It also fostered the growth of complex settlements characterized by organized streets, defensive fortifications, and communal spaces.

The establishment of sedentary settlements accelerated technological advancements that were closely tied to agriculture. These advancements included the development of plows and other implements, techniques for seed selection, and irrigation systems. These innovations improved harvesting methods and increased agricultural productivity, allowing for larger yields and supporting growing populations.

As settlements expanded, new social classes emerged. Warriors became essential to defend the villages against potential threats, while priests took on the role of conducting religious rituals aimed at safeguarding crops and protecting the community. Innovations like calendars and plows improved agricultural practices, and the invention of the wheel and the use of metal weapons and tools revolutionized daily life.

Additionally, this transition altered the dynamics between men and women. Men became more engaged in farming and herding, assuming responsibilities outside the settlement, while women remained behind, tending to children, weaving textiles, and performing other tasks that anchored them in one place.

A consequence of the Neolithic Revolution was the increased prevalence of disease compared to hunter-gather communities. Another negative change was the lack of free time. Overseeing farms and domesticating animals are labor intensive and require more people, time, and energy than hunting and gathering. Consequently, Neolithic humans had less free time in the day than people living in hunter-gather communities.

Important Social Changes

The transition to food production that happened between twenty thousand and five thousand years ago was a significant change in history. The transition from reliance on wild food sources to domestication was not a sudden and isolated event. Humans have been resourceful for a long time, so this transition likely involved building upon existing practices and making adjustments.

It is evident that the shift to agriculture led to increased work and potential health issues, so it is not clear why this change occurred. Many theories about the emergence of food production relate to changing environments. It is hypothesized that environmental changes could have reduced the number of resources in a region, prompting populations to adapt in various ways.

The correlation between food production and settlement patterns is evident. When people began domesticating animals, mobility decreased, leading to a more sedentary lifestyle. This sedentary lifestyle allowed people to invest more time in building structures. Additionally, the surplus generated by agriculture and pastoralism enabled larger populations to live together, resulting in larger settlements compared to foraging societies.

As food surplus continued to increase, new forms of settlements emerged. Changes in social and political systems are closely intertwined with food production. As the population increased because of settled communities based around farming, leadership became essential for coordinating group activities and establishing relations with other groups.

Over time, smelting and the use of copper tools emerged, allowing subsequent cultures to create bronze items. This period is, of course, called the Bronze Age. Around six thousand years ago, plows were introduced for farming. Tools and weapons like axes, swords, and plows could be made stronger and more resilient thanks to the development of metalworking. These inventions increased agricultural output, aided in land clearing, and strengthened defenses, allowing communities to defend their towns and expand their lands. The extraction and manipulation of metals also played a crucial role in the development of trade networks. The availability of metals, particularly bronze, created a demand for raw materials and facilitated long-distance trade. Communities with access to metal ores or the skills to produce bronze gained economic advantages, fostering the exchange of goods, ideas, and cultural practices.

This time period is characterized by more complex societies that developed through advancements in agriculture and metalworking. The settlements with surplus agricultural products and trade eventually gave rise to great civilizations in Egypt, Mesopotamia, China, and India. We will talk about these civilizations in the next chapter.

Chapter 9 – The Rise of the First States and Civilizations

The Neolithic Age laid the foundation for significant future changes. As people mastered agriculture, some villages progressed into more complex and prosperous societies. To safeguard their wealth, they constructed armies and city walls. By the onset of the Bronze Age, a considerable number of people inhabited the river valleys of Mesopotamia, Egypt, India, and China. These agricultural communities eventually developed into cities. Evidence indicates the existence of small permanent settlements and early agricultural practices around ten thousand to twelve thousand years ago, but fully developed city-states did not emerge until approximately five thousand years ago.

This period saw the emergence of societies we are familiar with today, characterized by large cities, autocratic rulers, bureaucracies, taxation, and formal judicial systems. The emergence of states in prehistory was driven by several key factors. The development of agriculture allowed for the sustenance of larger populations, creating the conditions for the establishment of settled communities. The food surplus gained from agriculture meant a need for storage and effective redistribution, which necessitated centralized authority. Centralized authority was also needed for defense against external threats.

The emergence of states also brought about significant cultural, technological, and economic advancements. Writing systems were developed to record laws, transactions, and historical events, enabling the preservation of knowledge and the dissemination of information. Monumental architecture, including temples and palaces, showcased the power and wealth of rulers while serving as symbols of societal identity.

After the advent of agriculture, human history witnessed a gradual but uneven consolidation of small-scale societies into the first states. This process was gradual and more complicated than it might sound.

Ancient civilizations laid the foundation for the complex societies and cultures that followed. These civilizations profoundly influenced the course of human history with their massive architecture, agricultural discoveries, governmental structures, and written languages.

Let us take a look at the earliest states and civilizations in the world.

Ancient Civilizations

The first states and ancient civilizations appeared in the Middle East along large rivers that allowed for the proper irrigation of crops. Soon after, ancient civilizations appeared around the world, typically around rivers. The early river valley civilizations developed independently, with each civilization based on the Agricultural Revolution of the Neolithic Age and the subsequent growth of cities. These civilizations shared common characteristics, including cities, government, religion, social structure, writing, and art. Water was the key to their success, as the villages and cities relied on a regular water supply for survival.

The first Mesopotamian civilizations include the following:

- Sumer. This civilization developed between the Tigris and Euphrates (in today's Iraq) between around 4500 and 4000 BCE. The Sumerians developed cities, often organized as city-states, such as Uruk. The Sumerian civilization also had a central administration, large temples, and effective irrigation. Sumer was also home to the first known writing system: cuneiform script.

- Akkad. Around 2300 BCE, this Mesopotamian empire reached its height of power. It was renowned for its kings and their conquests of neighboring lands. Around 2100 BCE, the Akkadian Empire fell.

- Assyria. This was a powerful empire that started out as a city-state and considerably expanded over the centuries. From its beginnings as an independent city-state around 2000 BCE,

Assyria expanded to include new territories, entering into conflict with other cultures, such as Babylonia and Egypt.

- Babylonia. Perhaps the best known of the Mesopotamian cultures, it was based in the city of Babylon. It expanded under the reign of Hammurabi (c. 1810–1750 BCE). Hammurabi is well known for his legal code, which was not the first legal code in history (although it was the first ancient Mesopotamian law code to be discovered).

Outside of Mesopotamia, early civilizations include the following:

- Ancient Egypt. Perhaps the most famous of all ancient civilizations, Egypt had a long history spanning around three thousand years. Located in the Nile Valley in northeast Africa, ancient Egypt is famous for its monumental architecture (the pyramids and great temples), its hieroglyphic writing, and rich artwork. Beginning with the unification of Upper and Lower Egypt in 3100 BCE, this civilization had its biggest success during the New Kingdom (from about 1550 to around 1069 BCE).

- Ancient India. Writing, huge urban centers, and extensive trade networks are hallmarks of the Indus River Valley civilization, which rose to prominence around 3300 BCE. Ancient India is famous for having one of the first examples of effective sewage systems.

- Ancient China. Chinese civilization is probably the longest-lasting of all in history. It traces its beginnings to the Shang dynasty, which had its beginnings around 1600 BC. It is known for early examples of Chinese writing, as well as powerful monarchs and a complex bureaucracy.[1]

- Minoan Civilization. This culture developed on the island of Crete (today's Greece) around 2000 BC from earlier Bronze Age communities. The Minoans had a writing system, lavishly decorated palaces (such as the one at Knossos), and rich trade around the Mediterranean. This civilization was followed by the Mycenaean civilization, which started around 1700 BCE.

---

[1] It is also possible that the Chinese civilization started even earlier with the Xia dynasty, around 2070 BCE.

- The Andean Civilization. The Andes region in South America was the birthplace of a diverse and complex civilization that developed around 3500 BCE. The Andean Plateau later reached its peak with the Inca Empire, the largest political system in the New World before the arrival of the Europeans.

- Olmec Civilization. It developed in Mesoamerica around 1200 BCE. The Olmecs built monumental architecture, established trade networks, and organized hierarchical social structures. This civilization is characterized by the creation of colossal stone heads depicting Olmec rulers.

- Maya Civilization. This is a Mesoamerican culture that developed around 2000 BCE. Between the years 750 and 500 BCE, they developed writing, formed complex societies, and built monumental architecture (step pyramids).

Sumerian writing; this tablet is for a bill of sale.
© *Marie-Lan Nguyen / Wikimedia Commons;*
https://commons.wikimedia.org/wiki/File:Bill_of_sale_Louvre_AO3766.jpg

Social Organization

A new social structure based on economic power emerged in these civilizations. Rulers and an upper class consisting of priests, government officials, and warriors dominated society. Below them was a large group of free individuals—farmers, artisans, and craftsmen—that occupied the middle of the social ladder. At the bottom of the social hierarchy was the slave class. The demands of the upper class for luxury goods spurred artisans and craftsmen to create new products, leading to organized trade and the transfer of technology between civilizations.

Warfare also contributed to the consolidation of power in early city-states. Warfare flourished alongside the development of large, concentrated cities, as living in such cities became more desirable due to the availability of resources for defense. Societies with larger populations and better-organized warfare capabilities outcompeted others, resulting in rapid expansion and conquests.

Governments organized and regulated activities, ensuring smooth interaction between individuals and groups. Monarchs typically led the governments of early civilizations. These rulers organized armies for protection and established laws to govern their subjects' lives. Another important social group in these early states was the priests. They played an important role not only in religious life but also in bureaucracy.

The storage and controlled distribution of surplus food allowed some members of society to specialize in occupations or social roles unrelated to food production. Still, rulers claimed the majority of wealth.

These early complex societies are considered the first examples of social stratification: a society in which different groups of people have different access to resources, wealth, and social positions. Unlike hunter-gatherer and early Neolithic groups, early states and civilizations were not egalitarian societies. City-states owed their existence to systemic inequalities between different groups in society.

Decline and Collapse

The early civilizations eventually declined and collapsed. Why? We still don't have a definite answer for all of them, although many theories have been proposed by experts to explain it. Explanations vary, with ecological factors often playing a role, from climate change to epidemic diseases. Another possible reason is warfare and internal social tensions.

States and civilizations often seek to expand, driven by surplus production, food security, trade, and population growth. Many times, their expansion was successful, transforming these societies into empires and military powers. However, this expansion made them more vulnerable to internal and external disturbances. Once destabilization began, the interdependence between institutions, castes, and economic sectors created tensions that were difficult to solve before the civilization collapsed.

Religion and ideology have also been implicated in the downfall of civilizations. Leaders redirecting resources toward religious rituals at the expense of subsistence led to food shortages and societal unrest. Blaming poor crop yields on perceived religious failings might have exacerbated resource allocation issues, ultimately leading to the collapse of a civilization.

Some scholars explain the collapse by the unnecessary complexity of bureaucracy in early civilizations. As societies become more complex, the costs of maintenance increase, with society requiring greater control and organization. This means more extensive networks, centralized control, and social stratification are needed. All of these things require a lot of human labor to sustain and organize, eventually leading to tensions within society.

The Importance of the First Civilizations

The rise of the first civilizations had a profound impact on the history of our species. The early states' achievements in agriculture, architecture, governance, law, and trade set benchmarks for future civilizations to build upon. The legacy of these ancient civilizations can still be seen in our modern institutions, legal systems, architectural designs, and cultural practices, reminding us of the enduring impact of these early civilizations.

The pyramids of Giza.

The development of sophisticated political structures was another significant benchmark. The demand for government and social order emerged as cultures evolved. The centralized power of monarchs or pharaohs, who controlled both politics and religion, helped early civilizations create hierarchical systems. These kings oversaw vast lands, organized labor, gathered taxes, and upheld law and order. The development of formal political institutions contributed to social cohesion and stability. Many governance structures today still bear the marks of these ancient political systems.

The first civilizations' economic systems also had a significant impact on the development of human communities. They conducted a significant amount of trade, both locally and over great distances. Cultural dispersion and economic expansion were facilitated by the exchange of goods and ideas. The emergence of economic systems based on specialization, currency, and markets—which remain the cornerstone of modern economies—was made possible by the establishment of trade routes and commercial hubs in ancient times.

Social stratification and inequalities are other aspects of early states that are still present in the world today. While we cannot fully compare today's societies with early civilizations, it is possible to talk about the effects of hierarchies and inequalities present in modern-day societies. Thus, many of the positive and negative characteristics of early states remain present in modern states.

The history of *Homo sapiens* is not complete without mentioning early civilizations. But that is all in the past now. In the book's final chapter, we will discuss the present, including the diversity of our species' cultures and biological makeup around the world.

Chapter 10 – Homo Sapiens Cultural and Biological Diversity

Since the first civilizations appeared millennia ago, humanity has performed remarkable exploits that have influenced the path of history. From its beginnings in prehistory, *Homo sapiens* has spread around the world, built villages and cities, and organized into small and larger groups.

Today, we can see these varied achievements around the globe. In this concluding chapter, we will talk about the cultural and biological diversity of *Homo sapiens* that exists in the world right now.

Homo Sapiens: A Biocultural Species

The extraordinary species known as *Homo sapiens* displays a complex array of biological and cultural variations. *Homo sapiens* populations across the world exhibit noticeable differences in physical characteristics and cultural practices while still being a part of the same species. To understand who we are as a species, we must look at both the biological and cultural sides of *Homo sapiens.*

The biocultural viewpoint emphasizes that our biology and culture coevolve and constantly influence and shape one another. Our biological evolution has resulted in cognitive abilities that promote learning, cooperation, and invention. It is critical to emphasize humanity's biological unity and the adaptations that have shaped our species while simultaneously diving into the concept of cultural variety.

Genetic adaptations to various settings led to biological diversity across human groups, and intricate interplay between sociocultural and environmental elements gave birth to cultural variation. For example, skin color is a visible trait in human populations. Biological anthropologists agree that skin color is adaptive and linked to the level of ultraviolet radiation (UVR) experienced by human populations in specific regions. It is crucial to note that similar skin colors have evolved independently in populations living in similar environments.

On the other hand, culture is a learned attribute that defines and shapes human societies. It is acquired through socialization, education, and experiences rather than being biologically determined.

A general definition of culture is the set of shared ideas, norms, and behaviors that define a given group or community. It is the filter through which people view the world and make sense of their experiences. Cultures exist within smaller groups like communities and organizations; it is not only limited to national or ethnic boundaries. It is a dynamic phenomenon that changes with time and adapts.

Cultural norms and values guide behavior by establishing acceptable standards of conduct and morality. Rituals, ceremonies, and social practices facilitate communal bonds, reinforcing a shared sense of identity. Artistic expressions reflect cultural values and aesthetics, serving as a reflection of the collective spirit of a society.

Cultural adaptations encompass the ways in which humans utilize knowledge to adapt and thrive in their environments. Through language, we can orally transmit or write ideas to help develop knowledge. Rather than reinventing the wheel in each generation, we compile and share knowledge. The advancements made in science and technology, including medicine, are products of culture. Instead of only wearing fur coats, we can start a fire, use a blanket, purchase a parka, or turn on the heat when we feel cold.

The formation of an identity at the individual and social level is greatly influenced by culture. It offers a framework for comprehending one's place in society, as well as a sense of belonging. Cultural identity includes both common and individual experiences, tying people to their origins and affecting how they view themselves. People frequently embrace their numerous cultural identities in multicultural communities, seeking methods to express and reconcile their varied roots.

Culture is a dynamic and shared phenomenon that is passed down through generations, shaping an individual's beliefs, values, and behaviors. Enculturation occurs through interaction with family members, adults, and peers, allowing individuals to internalize the cultural knowledge necessary for their participation in society.

Unlike genetic evolution, cultural evolution occurs at an accelerated pace and can rapidly shape human societies. The transmission of cultural information through social learning allows for the accumulation and refinement of knowledge, fostering innovation and adaptability. Cultural practices, such as agriculture, writing, and the development of complex social structures, have transformed the trajectory of human history, enabling us to thrive in diverse environments and overcome challenges.

Homo Sapiens Cultural Diversity

One of the main characteristics of *Homo sapiens* as a species is its remarkable cultural diversity. Cultures can be of various sizes and can either be concentrated in a specific region or spread across the world as diasporic communities.

The variety of cultural practices, beliefs, languages, social conventions, and customs that exist among various human groups is referred to as cultural diversity. It is a result of societal and environmental variables. Geographical position, temperature, resource accessibility, and exposure to various ecological circumstances are examples of environmental effects on culture. Historical occurrences, interpersonal interactions, migration, commerce, colonization, and the generational transfer of knowledge and customs are all examples of sociocultural forces.

There are universal traits and common human experiences that cut beyond cultural barriers, though. For instance, social organization, family systems, and belief systems have evolved in all human communities. All human communities share the essential needs for food, housing, social contact, and the quest for knowledge and meaning. However, the manner in which groups organize these things can be very different.

Since culture is learned, an individual is not born with inherent knowledge about how to be a fully functioning member of their society. They must acquire this knowledge through a process called enculturation. The primary transmitters of culture are typically parents, grandparents, or other close adults who have a lot of contact with infants and young children.

Culture is not a static concept but a dynamic one that constantly evolves. Societies continuously adapt and transform, and no culture remains unchanged as if it were a museum exhibit. Individuals possess the capacity to learn and incorporate new cultural elements, modify existing cultural practices, and adopt behaviors from other cultures. This process of cultural adaptation allows societies to respond to changing circumstances, embrace innovation, and evolve over time. The ability to learn and adapt is a testament to culture's learned nature, as it is driven by an individual's capacity for cognition, reflection, and integration of new knowledge into their cultural repertoire.

Homo Sapiens Biological Diversity

While we can easily perceive physical differences between humans, *Homo sapiens* is not a particularly diverse species in the biological sense. Despite the obvious distinctions that exist among *Homo sapiens* populations, there are underlying traits that connect our species together. All *Homo sapiens* have a common ancestor in terms of biology, as shown by our DNA. With an estimated 99.9 percent genetic similarity, the human genome is extremely similar across populations. This biological similarity emphasizes our common evolutionary past and the absence of a biological foundation for race.

The notion that all humans share approximately 99.9 percent of their genes highlights the biological unity of our species. Genetic diversity primarily arises at the individual level, with variations occurring within populations rather than between them. Recognizing and celebrating our shared genetic heritage can help dispel misconceptions and promote a more inclusive and egalitarian understanding of human diversity.

The most genetically varied continent is Africa, which is said to be the cradle of humanity. This seems reasonable given that all other humans are descended from *Homo sapiens* populations that left Africa in prehistoric times. Even this increased diversity in comparison to other human populations is still quite small. In fact, chimpanzees, our closest animal relatives, display much higher genetic diversity within their species than the entire of humanity.

In light of this, it is evident that attempting to classify people into races based on geographic patterns of biological variation between populations is destined to fail. The question of how many races exist is inherently flawed.

Race is a social construction rather than a biological fact. The concept of race is arbitrary in nature. Anthropologists face difficulties in classifying races due to the subjective selection of traits to define races. In other words, there is no objective way to define race as a human concept biologically since it does not correctly describe human biological variation. The concept of race assumes the existence of three to five (or another arbitrary number) distinct groups within the *Homo sapiens* species.

However, this is not how human biological variation works. Identical physical traits can appear in different groups, even if they are more prevalent in one group than others. For example, blue eyes and blond hair appear naturally in people of all races. Moreover, most traits used to define race exhibit continuous variation, which means they display gradual and not sharp differences. This poses challenges when attempting to divide a continuous curve into distinct groups. For example, skin color is often seen as a prime racial trait, but it shows continuous variation within and between populations, making it difficult to determine where to draw the line between "dark" and "light" races. Defining races based on traits with continuous variation is arbitrary and subjective and lacks scientific validity.

There is a biological unity of our species, *Homo sapiens*. We are very similar to each other when it comes to genetics.

Similarities and Differences between Us

The exploration of human biological and cultural diversity reveals both striking similarities and intriguing differences among *Homo sapiens* groups. Sociocultural and environmental elements work together to produce cultural diversity. The emergence of various cultural practices, languages, and social conventions is influenced by geography, historical events, migratory patterns, and contacts between various human groups. Cultural variety can exist inside local communities and subcultures, as well as across national and ethnic boundaries.

The fact that *Homo sapiens* exhibit both biological homogeneity and cultural variation highlights the intricate connection between biology and culture. While the cognitive abilities that support cultural learning, cooperation, and creativity have been bequeathed to us by biological evolution, our social identities and behaviors are also shaped by cultural practices, beliefs, and values.

The study of human biological and cultural diversity underscores the intricacies of *Homo sapiens*. It highlights our common genetic ancestry and the vast array of cultural expressions that enrich our societies. By exploring these dimensions of diversity, we gain valuable insights into who we are as a species and foster a deeper appreciation for the multifaceted nature of human existence.

Conclusion – The Legacy of Our Species

The journey of *Homo sapiens* has been an extraordinary one. From humble beginnings in Africa, our ancestors embarked on a path of evolution, survival, and innovation that ultimately led to the dominance of our species on Earth. Throughout this book, we have explored the origins of *Homo sapiens* and delved into the factors that contributed to our success and resilience as a species.

The story of human evolution begins with the earliest hominins, those displaying signs of developing bipedalism. Bipedalism played a crucial role in hominin evolution. Walking on two legs proved efficient, allowing hominins to save energy compared to four-legged primates. Bipedalism also facilitated better detection of potential dangers and food sources while freeing up hands for tool use. In this book, we highlighted the importance of early hominins, as well as early human species, prior to the emergence of *Homo sapiens*, such as *Homo erectus*, *Homo heidelbergensis*, and the Neanderthals.

We followed the appearance of our species, *Homo sapiens sapiens*, from its beginnings 300,000 years ago. The earliest *Homo sapiens* fossils in Africa and subsequent migrations out of the continent shaped the spread of our species. The emergence of *Homo sapiens* brought advancements in tool production and cultural practices, along with rapid population growth.

The age of migrations, marked by the movement of *Homo sapiens* across the globe, was a complex and dynamic process. Throughout these migrations, *Homo sapiens* faced challenges and exhibited remarkable adaptability. They developed innovative strategies to survive in diverse environments. Technological advancements, such as tailored clothing and food storage techniques, contributed to their success. As *Homo sapiens* settled in new regions, they developed distinct cultures, languages, art forms, and social systems.

The development of human cognition allowed early humans to form strong social groups and master toolmaking, enhancing their chances of survival. Additionally, language development enabled more effective and sophisticated communication, serving as a universal trait that unites all human beings and facilitates cross-cultural interaction despite the vast diversity of cultural experiences worldwide.

The prehistoric period encompassed a vast span of time before the advent of written records. During this era, *Homo sapiens* developed essential skills and technologies that laid the foundation for future advancements. The mastery of fire, for instance, revolutionized human existence by providing warmth, cooked food, and protection from predators. It also served as a catalyst for social cohesion, as early humans gathered around fires to share stories and foster social bonds.

The invention of tools was another pivotal achievement. From simple stone tools to more complex implements, humans gradually refined their ability to manipulate their environment. This development enabled them to hunt, gather, and eventually cultivate crops, leading to the emergence of settled agricultural communities.

Throughout history, *Homo sapiens* have showcased a rich cultural heritage. Their artistic expressions, from cave paintings to literature, provide a glimpse into their beliefs and understanding of the world. The cave paintings, which were created thousands of years ago, serve as a testament to the artistic impulse that resided within early humans. These remarkable artworks provide glimpses into their daily lives, hunting practices, and mythological beliefs.

Around 10,000 BCE, humans experienced a transformative shift with the transition from a nomadic hunter-gatherer lifestyle to settled agricultural communities. This marked the Agricultural Revolution, a pivotal milestone in human history.

The progression of human civilization was closely intertwined with technological advancements. The Bronze Age, characterized by the use of bronze tools and weapons, witnessed significant strides in metallurgy. This era marked a transition from stone tools to more durable and versatile metal implements, revolutionizing warfare, trade, and craftsmanship.

States and civilizations brought about significant cultural, technological, and economic advancements. Writing systems were developed to record laws, transactions, and historical events, enabling the preservation and dissemination of knowledge. Monumental architecture, such as temples and palaces, showcased the power and wealth of rulers while serving as symbols of societal identity.

The rise of the first civilizations had a profound impact on human history. Their achievements in agriculture, architecture, governance, law, and trade set benchmarks for future civilizations. The legacy of these ancient civilizations can still be observed in modern institutions, legal systems, architectural designs, and cultural practices.

The Future

So, what's in store for the future of our species? It is not always easy to tell, but we can come up with some ideas. The legacy of *Homo sapiens* is deeply intertwined with the ability to invent and utilize tools. From the invention of the wheel to the development of computers, our technological prowess has propelled us forward. The Agricultural Revolution allowed us to settle in one place and create civilizations, while the Industrial Revolution revolutionized manufacturing and transportation. It is likely that technology in the Digital Revolution will continue to hold importance for *Homo sapiens* in the future.

Artificial intelligence advancements could result in unprecedented levels of automation, altering businesses and the labor market. While this may cause substantial societal disruption, it also provides humans with an opportunity to pursue more creative, meaningful endeavors. The responsible development and regulation of emerging technologies will be paramount in mitigating risks and ensuring that progress benefits all of humanity.

In terms of biological evolution, *Homo sapiens* may continue to undergo gradual changes, albeit at a slower pace compared to technological advancements. Genetic engineering, gene editing, and reproductive technologies offer the potential to manipulate our own genetic makeup. While this raises ethical concerns, it also opens doors to eliminating genetic diseases and enhancing certain traits.

Societal transformation will also be a crucial aspect of our future. Science, cultural interchange, and the collective drive for progress will all affect the evolution of societal values and norms.

We are beings endowed with rationality, consciousness, and a capacity for emotional connection. We communicate through language, celebrate our cultural diversity, and express our creativity. Recognizing and celebrating our shared genetic heritage can foster inclusivity and a more accurate understanding of human diversity. While our cultural practices and beliefs may differ, there is a biological unity that connects all *Homo sapiens.*

Here's another book by Captivating History that you might like

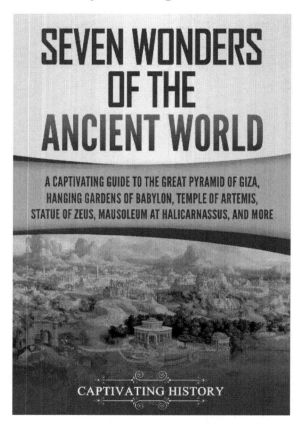

Free Bonus from Captivating History (Available for a Limited time)

Hi History Lovers!

Now you have a chance to join our exclusive history list so you can get your first history ebook for free as well as discounts and a potential to get more history books for free! Simply visit the link below to join.

Captivatinghistory.com/ebook

Also, make sure to follow us on Facebook, Twitter and Youtube by searching for Captivating History.

References

Alex Mesoudi and Kenichi Aoki (eds). *Learning Strategies and Cultural Evolution during the Palaeolithic*. 2015.

Bernard Wood. *Human Evolution: A Very Short Introduction*. 2005.

Chris Godsen. *Prehistory: A Very Short Introduction*. 2003.

Clive Finlayson. *The Humans Who Went Extinct: Why the Neanderthals Died Out and We Survived*. 2009.

Peter Gardenfors. *How Homo Became Sapiens: The Evolution of Thinking*. 2006.

Silvana Condemi and François Savatier. *A Pocket History of Human Evolution: How We Became Sapiens*. 2019.

Yuval Noah Harari. *Sapiens: A Brief History of Humankind*. 2014.

Made in United States
Orlando, FL
09 October 2023

37717796R00061